Grade

KUMON MATH WORKBOOKS

Pre-Algebra
Workbook 1

Table of Contents

No.	Title	Page
1.	Fraction Review	2
2.	Reduction Review	4
3.	Greatest Common Factor	6
4.	Comparing Fractions	8
5.	Least Common Multiple	10
6.	Comparing Fractions	12
7.	Addition of Fractions	14
8.	Addition of Fractions	16
9.	Addition of Fractions	18
10.	Subtraction of Fractions	20
11.	Subtraction of Fractions	22
12.	Addition & Subtraction of Fractions	24
13.	Word Problems with Fractions	26
14.	Multiplication of Fractions	28
15.	Multiplication of Fractions	30
16.	Division of Fractions	32
17.	Division of Fractions	34
18.	Word Problems with Fractions	36
19.	Fraction Review	38
20.	Place Value Review	40
21.	Decimals as Fractions	42
22.	Fractions as Decimals	44
23.	Percents	46

No.	Title	Page
24.	Percents	48
25.	Percents	50
26.	Decimals and Fractions	52
27.	Decimals and Fractions	54
28.	Word Problems with Decimals and Fractions	56
29.	Exponents	58
30.	Exponents	60
31.	Order of Operations	62
32.	Order of Operations	64
33.	Order of Operations	66
34.	Order of Operations	68
35.	Order of Operations	70
36.	Word Problems with Order of Operations	72
37.	Order of Operations	74
38.	Order of Operations	76
39.	Order of Operations	78
40.	Order of Operations	80
41.	Order of Operations	82
42.	Review	84
43.	Review	86
	Answer Key	88

KUMON

Fraction Review

1 Rewrite each improper fraction as a mixed number or whole number.   2 points per question

(1) $\dfrac{5}{4} =$ $1\dfrac{1}{4}$

(2) $\dfrac{7}{5} =$ $1\dfrac{2}{5}$

(3) $\dfrac{4}{4} =$ 1

(4) $\dfrac{7}{3} =$ $2\dfrac{1}{3}$

(5) $\dfrac{7}{4} =$ $1\dfrac{3}{4}$

(6) $\dfrac{6}{3} =$ 2

(7) $\dfrac{5}{2} =$ $4\dfrac{1}{2}$

(8) $\dfrac{9}{4} =$ $2\dfrac{1}{4}$

(9) $\dfrac{10}{3} =$ $3\dfrac{1}{3}$

(10) $\dfrac{15}{11} =$ $1\dfrac{4}{11}$

(11) $\dfrac{9}{9} =$ 1

(12) $\dfrac{13}{7} =$ $1\dfrac{6}{7}$

(13) $\dfrac{14}{7} =$ 2

(14) $\dfrac{12}{3} =$ 4

(15) $\dfrac{11}{4} =$ $2\dfrac{3}{4}$

(16) $\dfrac{13}{3} =$ $4\dfrac{1}{3}$

(17) $\dfrac{15}{7} =$ $2\dfrac{1}{7}$

(18) $\dfrac{3}{1} =$ 1

(19) $\dfrac{17}{9} =$ $9\dfrac{8}{9}$

(20) $\dfrac{18}{7} =$ $2\dfrac{4}{7}$

2 Rewrite each whole number as a fraction.

3 points per question

(1) $1 = \dfrac{4}{4}$

(2) $1 = \dfrac{7}{7}$

(3) $2 = \dfrac{10}{5}$

(4) $2 = \dfrac{14}{7}$

(5) $3 = \dfrac{3}{3}$

(6) $3 = \dfrac{12}{4}$

(7) $1 = \dfrac{9}{9}$

(8) $2 = \dfrac{16}{8}$

3 Rewrite each mixed number as an improper fraction.

3 points per question

(1) $1\dfrac{1}{2} = \dfrac{3}{2}$

(2) $1\dfrac{4}{5} = \dfrac{9}{5}$

(3) $2\dfrac{4}{5} = \dfrac{14}{5}$

(4) $2\dfrac{5}{6} = \dfrac{17}{6}$

(5) $1\dfrac{4}{7} = \dfrac{11}{7}$

(6) $2\dfrac{1}{3} = \dfrac{7}{3}$

(7) $4\dfrac{2}{3} = \dfrac{14}{3}$

(8) $1\dfrac{7}{13} = \dfrac{20}{13}$

(9) $3\dfrac{5}{11} = \dfrac{38}{11}$

(10) $2\dfrac{1}{8} = \dfrac{17}{8}$

(11) $1\dfrac{4}{11} = \dfrac{15}{11}$

(12) $5\dfrac{3}{4} = \dfrac{23}{4}$

A fraction such as $\dfrac{3}{2}$, whose numerator is greater than the denominator is called an improper fraction.

Great start!

2 Reduction Review

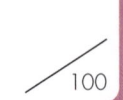

1. Reduce by dividing the numerator and denominator by 2, 3, or 5.

2 points per question

(1) $\dfrac{3}{6} = \dfrac{1}{2}$

(2) $\dfrac{5}{15} =$

(3) $\dfrac{12}{15} =$

(4) $\dfrac{14}{20} =$

(5) $\dfrac{21}{30} =$

2. Reduce by dividing the numerator and denominator by 2, 3, or 7.

2 points per question

(1) $\dfrac{7}{21} =$

(2) $\dfrac{12}{14} =$

(3) $\dfrac{21}{35} =$

(4) $\dfrac{12}{21} =$

(5) $\dfrac{30}{33} =$

Reduction means simplifying a fraction by dividing the numerator and denominator by the same number.

3 Reduce.

4 points per question

Example $\frac{16}{28} = \frac{8}{14} = \frac{4}{7}$

(1) $\frac{8}{16} =$

(2) $\frac{12}{16} = \frac{6}{12} \frac{3}{6} \frac{1}{2}$

(3) $\frac{25}{35} = \frac{4}{7}$

(4) $\frac{15}{21} = \frac{3}{7}$

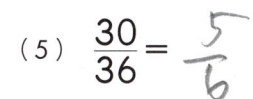

(5) $\frac{30}{36} = \frac{5}{6}$

(6) $\frac{10}{30} = \frac{1}{3}$

(7) $\frac{20}{44} = \frac{10}{22} \frac{5}{11}$

(8) $\frac{14}{56} = \frac{7}{28}$

You may want to reduce more than once.

4 Reduce.

4 points per question

(1) $\frac{12}{20} = \frac{6}{10} \frac{3}{5}$

(2) $\frac{20}{24} = \frac{10}{12} = \frac{5}{6}$

(3) $\frac{8}{56} = \frac{4}{28} = \frac{1}{14}$

(4) $\frac{14}{28} = \frac{7}{14} = \frac{1}{2}$

(5) $\frac{12}{36} = \frac{6}{6} = 1$

(6) $\frac{25}{50} = \frac{5}{10}$

(7) $\frac{9}{21} = \frac{3}{7}$

(8) $\frac{28}{60} = \frac{14}{30} = \frac{7}{15}$

(9) $\frac{25}{75} = \frac{5}{15} = \frac{1}{3}$

(10) $\frac{22}{66} = \frac{11}{33}$

(11) $\frac{18}{45} = \frac{6}{15}$

(12) $\frac{21}{56} = \frac{3}{8}$

Try to reduce each fraction in one step.

If you have to reduce in more than one step, just keep practicing. You'll get it!

3 Greatest Common Factor

Don't forget!
8 can be divided evenly by 1, 2, 4, and 8. This means that 1, 2, 4, and 8 are **factors** of 8.

1 Write the appropriate number in each box.   4 points per question

(1) The factors of 16 are … 1, 2, 4, [8], 16
(2) The factors of 20 are … 1, 2, 4, [ ], 10, 20
(3) The common factors of 16 and 20 are … 1, 2, [ ]
(4) The factors of 12 are … 1, 2, 3, 4, [ ], 12
(5) The factors of 24 are … 1, 2, 3, 4, 6, 8, [ ], 24
(6) The common factors of 12 and 24 are … 1, 2, 3, 4, [ ], 12

Don't forget!
The factors that two or more integers have in common are called **common factors**.

2 Write the appropriate number in each box.   2 points per question

(1) The greatest common factor of 16 and 20 is [4].
(2) The greatest common factor of 12 and 24 is [ ].

Don't forget!
Among the common factors, the largest factor that two integers have in common is called the **greatest common factor (GCF)**.

3 Write the GCF of each number pair.   3 points per question

Example (16, 20) → [4]

(1) (12, 30) → [ ]   (3) (14, 42) → [ ]
(2) (20, 45) → [ ]   (4) (45, 54) → [ ]

2 Compare each pair of fractions.   5 points per question

(1) $\frac{20}{30}$, $\frac{20}{60}$

$\frac{\square}{3} \square \frac{\square}{3}$

(2) $\frac{18}{45}$, $\frac{10}{25}$

$\frac{\square}{\square}$

(3) $\frac{8}{32}$, $\frac{12}{16}$

$\frac{\square}{\square}$

(4) $\frac{24}{52}$, $\frac{6}{39}$

$\frac{\square}{\square}$

(5) $\frac{50}{80}$, $\frac{24}{64}$

$\frac{\square}{\square}$

(6) $\frac{32}{56}$, $\frac{12}{21}$

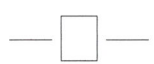

$\frac{\square}{\square}$

To compare two fractions, first make their denominators equal.

3 Answer each word problem.   15 points per question

(1) Amanda has $\frac{15}{16}$ pound of beads. Tessa has $\frac{24}{32}$ pound of beads. Who has more beads?

$\frac{15}{16}$, $\frac{24}{32}$ → $\frac{\square}{\square}$

⟨Ans.⟩ _____

(2) Leslie ate $\frac{12}{36}$ pint of blueberries. Joey ate $\frac{18}{27}$ pint of strawberries. Who ate more fruit?

⟨Ans.⟩ _____

Brilliant work!

5 Least Common Multiple

Date / / Name Level ★ Score /100

1 Write the multiples of 4 in ascending order. — 4 points for completion

4, 8, 12, 16, ☐, ☐, ☐, ☐, ☐, ...

2 Write the multiples of 6 in ascending order. — 4 points for completion

6, 12, 18, ☐, ☐, ☐, ☐, ☐, ☐, ...

3 Write the multiples of 7 in ascending order. — 4 points for completion

7, 14, ☐, ☐, ☐, ☐, ☐, ☐, ☐, ...

4 Write the multiples of 9 in ascending order. — 4 points for completion

9, ☐, ☐, ☐, ☐, ☐, ☐, ☐, ☐, ...

5 Write the common multiples of 4 and 6 in ascending order. — 4 points for completion

12, ☐, ☐, ...

> **Don't forget!**
> The multiples that two integers have in common are called **common multiples**.

6 Write the common multiples of 6 and 9 in ascending order. — 4 points for completion

☐, ☐, ☐, ...

> **Don't forget!**
> The smallest common multiple is called the **least common multiple (LCM)**.

7 Write the common multiples of 4 and 7 in ascending order. — 4 points for completion

☐, ...

8 Write the appropriate number in each box.

2 points per question

(1) The least common multiple of 4 and 6 is ...

(2) The least common multiple of 6 and 9 is ...

(3) The least common multiple of 4 and 7 is ...

(4) The least common multiple of 4 and 9 is ...

9 Find the LCM of each number pair.

4 points per question

Example (4, 6) → 12

(1) (6, 8) →

(2) (4, 10) →

(3) (2, 9) →

(4) (6, 12) →

(5) (3, 8) →

(6) (3, 4) →

(7) (8, 12) →

(8) (5, 7) →

(9) (9, 12) →

(10) (6, 10) →

(11) (7, 8) →

(12) (9, 15) →

(13) (3, 11) →

(14) (2, 7) →

(15) (7, 9) →

(16) (5, 12) →

Remarkable job!

6 Comparing Fractions

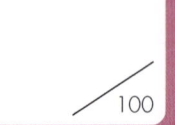

1 Find the LCM of the denominators in each pair of fractions. Then compare the fractions.

5 points per question

(1) $\frac{1}{3}, \frac{2}{4}$ — The LCM of 3 and 4 is $\boxed{12}$.

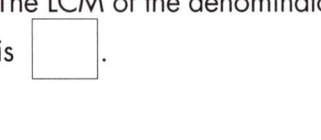

$\frac{\boxed{4}}{12} \boxed{<} \frac{\boxed{6}}{12}$

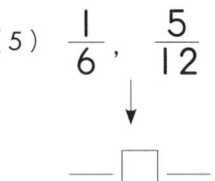

(2) $\frac{3}{4}, \frac{7}{10}$ — The LCM of the denominators is $\boxed{20}$.

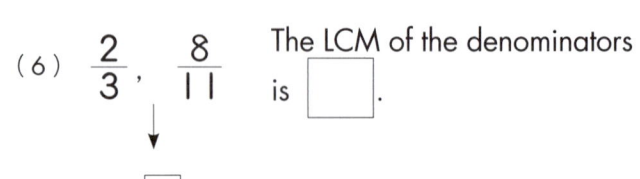

$\frac{\boxed{}}{\boxed{}} \boxed{\phantom{<}} \frac{\boxed{}}{\boxed{}}$

(3) $\frac{3}{8}, \frac{5}{12}$ — The LCM of the denominators is $\boxed{}$.

$\frac{\boxed{}}{\boxed{}} \boxed{\phantom{<}} \frac{\boxed{}}{\boxed{}}$

(4) $\frac{2}{5}, \frac{6}{7}$ — The LCM of the denominators is $\boxed{}$.

$\frac{\boxed{}}{\boxed{}} \boxed{\phantom{<}} \frac{\boxed{}}{\boxed{}}$

(5) $\frac{1}{6}, \frac{5}{12}$ — The LCM of the denominators is $\boxed{}$.

$\frac{\boxed{}}{\boxed{}} \boxed{\phantom{<}} \frac{\boxed{}}{\boxed{}}$

(6) $\frac{2}{3}, \frac{8}{11}$ — The LCM of the denominators is $\boxed{}$.

$\frac{\boxed{}}{\boxed{}} \boxed{\phantom{<}} \frac{\boxed{}}{\boxed{}}$

(7) $\frac{4}{5}, \frac{7}{12}$ — The LCM of the denominators is $\boxed{}$.

$\frac{\boxed{}}{\boxed{}} \boxed{\phantom{<}} \frac{\boxed{}}{\boxed{}}$

(8) $\frac{4}{5}, \frac{9}{10}$ — The LCM of the denominators is $\boxed{}$.

$\frac{\boxed{}}{\boxed{}} \boxed{\phantom{<}} \frac{\boxed{}}{\boxed{}}$

To compare two fractions, first make their denominators equal.

2 Compare each pair of fractions.   5 points per question

(1) $\frac{1}{4}, \frac{5}{6}$ —☐—

(2) $\frac{3}{5}, \frac{7}{9}$ —☐—

(3) $\frac{8}{9}, \frac{12}{15}$ —☐—

(4) $\frac{5}{6}, \frac{7}{9}$ —☐—

(5) $\frac{3}{4}, \frac{3}{7}$ —☐—

(6) $\frac{1}{2}, \frac{3}{13}$ —☐—

3 Answer each word problem.   15 points per question

(1) Sarah is $\frac{5}{7}$ as tall as her mother. Her sister Leah is $\frac{10}{11}$ as tall as their mother. Who is taller, Leah or Sarah?

⟨Ans.⟩ _____

(2) Mr. Hall's gym class is $\frac{3}{4}$ full. Mrs. Castamore's dance class is $\frac{8}{9}$ full. Who's class is more full?

⟨Ans.⟩ _____

You can compare any fractions! Well done!

Addition of Fractions

1 Add. *3 points per question*

Examples $\frac{3}{8}+\frac{3}{8}=\frac{6}{8}=\frac{3}{4}$ $\frac{3}{8}+\frac{5}{8}=\frac{8}{8}=1$ $\frac{7}{8}+\frac{3}{8}=\frac{10}{8}=1\frac{2}{8}=1\frac{1}{4}$

(1) $\frac{3}{5}+\frac{1}{5}=$

(2) $\frac{5}{8}+\frac{3}{8}=\frac{8}{8}=$

(3) $\frac{5}{7}+\frac{4}{7}=\frac{9}{7}=$

(4) $\frac{5}{9}+\frac{8}{9}=$

(5) $\frac{5}{6}+\frac{5}{6}=\frac{10}{6}=1\frac{4}{6}=$

(6) $\frac{7}{12}+\frac{11}{12}=$

(7) $\frac{7}{9}+\frac{1}{9}=$

(8) $\frac{6}{11}+\frac{7}{11}=$

(9) $\frac{9}{13}+\frac{4}{13}=$

(10) $\frac{11}{12}+\frac{5}{12}=$

(11) $\frac{9}{10}+\frac{9}{10}=$

(12) $\frac{7}{8}+\frac{5}{8}=$

Always reduce and write your answers as proper fractions.

2 Find the LCM of the denominators in each pair of fractions.   4 points per question

(1) $\frac{1}{6}, \frac{8}{9}$ → 18

(2) $\frac{2}{3}, \frac{2}{5}$ →

(3) $\frac{1}{4}, \frac{5}{9}$ →

(4) $\frac{5}{6}, \frac{2}{15}$ →

(5) $\frac{3}{4}, \frac{13}{16}$ →

(6) $\frac{4}{5}, \frac{5}{6}$ →

(7) $\frac{3}{8}, \frac{7}{10}$ →

(8) $\frac{1}{6}, \frac{13}{14}$ →

(9) $\frac{3}{10}, \frac{12}{15}$ →

(10) $\frac{8}{9}, \frac{5}{12}$ →

3 Find the LCM and then use it to add the fractions.   4 points per question

(1) (3, 4) → 12

$\frac{1}{3} + \frac{1}{4} = \frac{4}{12} + \frac{3}{12} =$

(2) (8, 12) →

$\frac{3}{8} + \frac{5}{12} =$

(3) (7, 8) →

$\frac{3}{7} + \frac{3}{8} =$

(4) (4, 9) →

$\frac{1}{4} + \frac{5}{9} =$

(5) (6, 8) →

$\frac{5}{6} + \frac{1}{8} =$

(6) (9, 15) →

$\frac{7}{9} + \frac{2}{15} =$

This is tough work, but you are doing great.

8 Addition of Fractions

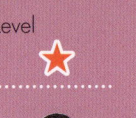

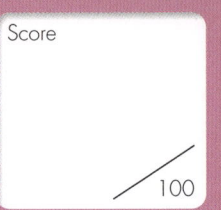

1 Find the LCM of the denominators of the fractions and then add.

4 points per question

Example $\frac{1}{3}+\frac{1}{7}=\frac{7}{21}+\frac{3}{21}=\frac{10}{21}$

(1) $\frac{2}{3}+\frac{1}{7}=$

(2) $\frac{3}{5}+\frac{1}{6}=$

(3) $\frac{5}{8}+\frac{3}{7}=$

(4) $\frac{5}{7}+\frac{5}{6}=$

(5) $\frac{5}{7}+\frac{4}{5}=$

(6) $\frac{7}{12}+\frac{1}{3}=$

(7) $\frac{4}{9}+\frac{1}{6}=$

(8) $\frac{4}{5}+\frac{3}{8}=$

(9) $\frac{1}{6}+\frac{5}{12}=$

(10) $\frac{11}{12}+\frac{5}{8}=$

(11) $\frac{3}{4}+\frac{2}{7}=$

(12) $\frac{3}{5}+\frac{7}{10}=$

2 Add.

4 points per question

(1) $\dfrac{4}{5} + \dfrac{1}{3} =$

(2) $\dfrac{2}{15} + \dfrac{7}{10} =$

(3) $\dfrac{2}{3} + \dfrac{6}{7} =$

(4) $\dfrac{5}{8} + \dfrac{1}{2} =$

(5) $\dfrac{11}{12} + \dfrac{1}{8} =$

(6) $\dfrac{3}{8} + \dfrac{5}{12} =$

(7) $\dfrac{3}{4} + \dfrac{2}{3} =$

(8) $\dfrac{1}{5} + \dfrac{1}{4} =$

(9) $\dfrac{3}{5} + \dfrac{9}{10} =$

(10) $\dfrac{3}{8} + \dfrac{1}{7} =$

(11) $\dfrac{4}{7} + \dfrac{1}{6} =$

(12) $\dfrac{1}{3} + \dfrac{8}{15} =$

(13) $\dfrac{1}{8} + \dfrac{3}{4} =$

Find the LCM of the denominators before adding.

Aim for perfection!

9 Addition of Fractions

1 Add.

5 points per question

(1) $\frac{1}{6} + \frac{1}{3} + \frac{1}{2} = \frac{\square}{12} + \frac{\square}{12} + \frac{\square}{12}$
$= \frac{\square}{12} =$

(2) $\frac{1}{2} + \frac{3}{5} + \frac{1}{3} =$

(3) $\frac{4}{9} + \frac{1}{3} + \frac{5}{6} =$

(4) $\frac{4}{5} + \frac{2}{3} + \frac{11}{15} =$

(5) $\frac{4}{9} + \frac{2}{3} + \frac{5}{6} =$

(6) $\frac{2}{3} + \frac{1}{5} + \frac{1}{4} =$

(7) $\frac{3}{4} + \frac{1}{9} + \frac{1}{6} =$

(8) $\frac{3}{8} + \frac{4}{5} + \frac{1}{4} =$

(9) $\frac{3}{11} + \frac{3}{4} + \frac{1}{2} =$

(10) $\frac{1}{2} + \frac{2}{5} + \frac{3}{10} =$

Find the LCM of the denominators before adding two or more fractions with different denominators.

2 Add.

5 points per question

(1) $\dfrac{3}{5}+\dfrac{1}{2}+\dfrac{5}{6}=$

(2) $1\dfrac{1}{2}+3\dfrac{3}{4}+\dfrac{1}{8}=1\dfrac{\square}{8}+3\dfrac{\square}{8}+\dfrac{1}{8}$

$=$

(3) $1\dfrac{5}{12}+\dfrac{3}{4}+1\dfrac{1}{2}=$

(4) $1\dfrac{3}{10}+2\dfrac{1}{7}+\dfrac{2}{5}=$

(5) $1\dfrac{4}{5}+3\dfrac{3}{8}+4\dfrac{1}{4}=$

(6) $1\dfrac{1}{3}+2\dfrac{3}{4}+\dfrac{3}{8}=$

(7) $2\dfrac{1}{2}+\dfrac{3}{4}+1\dfrac{5}{6}=$

(8) $\dfrac{2}{3}+1\dfrac{1}{4}+2\dfrac{1}{6}=$

(9) $1\dfrac{3}{4}+\dfrac{1}{6}+2\dfrac{2}{9}=$

(10) $\dfrac{5}{6}+1\dfrac{3}{8}+1\dfrac{5}{12}=$

If you are having difficulty adding fractions, try Kumon's *Grade 6 Fractions* workbook for extra practice.

You are great at adding fractions!

10 Subtraction of Fractions

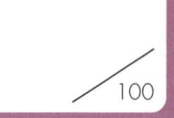

1 Subtract.

5 points per question

(1) $\dfrac{3}{7} - \dfrac{1}{7} = \dfrac{2}{7}$

(2) $\dfrac{3}{4} - \dfrac{1}{4} =$

(3) $\dfrac{5}{6} - \dfrac{1}{6} =$

(4) $\dfrac{8}{13} - \dfrac{3}{13} =$

(5) $\dfrac{9}{11} - \dfrac{4}{11} =$

(6) $\dfrac{4}{5} - \dfrac{3}{5} =$

(7) $\dfrac{7}{12} - \dfrac{5}{12} =$

(8) $\dfrac{11}{15} - \dfrac{6}{15} =$

(9) $\dfrac{17}{20} - \dfrac{11}{20} =$

(10) $\dfrac{23}{24} - \dfrac{13}{24} =$

Don't forget to reduce your answer whenever possible.

2 Subtract.

5 points per question

(1) $\dfrac{2}{3} - \dfrac{1}{4} = \dfrac{8}{12} - \dfrac{3}{12} =$

(2) $\dfrac{7}{12} - \dfrac{1}{3} =$

(3) $\dfrac{7}{11} - \dfrac{1}{2} =$

(4) $2\dfrac{7}{11} - 1\dfrac{1}{2} = 2\dfrac{\Box}{22} - 1\dfrac{\Box}{22} =$

(5) $3\dfrac{5}{7} - 1\dfrac{1}{3} =$

(6) $4\dfrac{7}{12} - 2\dfrac{1}{2} =$

(7) $2\dfrac{3}{5} - 1\dfrac{3}{10} =$

(8) $3\dfrac{3}{4} - 1\dfrac{5}{12} =$

(9) $2\dfrac{4}{9} - \dfrac{1}{6} =$

(10) $3\dfrac{5}{6} - 2\dfrac{3}{10} =$

Find the LCM of the denominators before subtracting two or more fractions with different denominators.

You make subtracting fractions look easy!

Subtraction of Fractions

1 Subtract.

Don't forget!
You can borrow from the whole number if the numerator of a mixed number is not large enough.

Example $3\frac{3}{4} - \frac{4}{5} = 3\frac{15}{20} - \frac{16}{20} = 2\frac{35}{20} - \frac{16}{20} = 2\frac{19}{20}$

5 points per question

(1) $3\frac{1}{4} - 1\frac{3}{5} = 3\frac{\square}{20} - 1\frac{\square}{20}$
$= 2\frac{\square}{20} - 1\frac{\square}{20} =$

(2) $5\frac{1}{3} - 2\frac{3}{7} =$

(3) $6\frac{2}{7} - 2\frac{1}{2} =$

(4) $7\frac{1}{2} - 4\frac{4}{5} =$

(5) $8\frac{1}{11} - 5\frac{1}{2} =$

(6) $3\frac{5}{13} - 1\frac{1}{2} =$

(7) $9\frac{1}{2} - 4\frac{11}{16} =$

(8) $4\frac{4}{11} - 3\frac{3}{4} =$

(9) $2\frac{1}{7} - \frac{11}{14} =$

(10) $1\frac{1}{4} - \frac{9}{10} =$

2 Subtract.

5 points per question

(1) $\dfrac{11}{12} - \dfrac{1}{4} - \dfrac{1}{3} = \dfrac{\square}{12} - \dfrac{\square}{12} - \dfrac{\square}{12}$

$=$

(2) $\dfrac{13}{14} - \dfrac{1}{2} - \dfrac{2}{7} =$

(3) $3\dfrac{7}{8} - 1\dfrac{1}{4} - \dfrac{1}{3} =$

(4) $7\dfrac{1}{8} - 2\dfrac{2}{3} - 1\dfrac{1}{6} =$

(5) $10\dfrac{7}{10} - 4\dfrac{1}{5} - \dfrac{3}{4} =$

(6) $9\dfrac{2}{9} - 3\dfrac{1}{2} - 3\dfrac{1}{3} =$

(7) $5\dfrac{7}{8} - 2\dfrac{1}{2} - 1\dfrac{1}{3} =$

(8) $4\dfrac{3}{4} - 1\dfrac{1}{6} - \dfrac{3}{8} =$

(9) $5\dfrac{3}{4} - 1\dfrac{4}{9} - 2\dfrac{1}{6} =$

(10) $3\dfrac{3}{8} - \dfrac{5}{6} - 1\dfrac{2}{3} =$

Always calculate from left to right.

I'm impressed!

12 Addition & Subtraction of Fractions

1 Calculate.   5 points per question

(1) $\dfrac{4}{9} + \dfrac{1}{2} - \dfrac{2}{3} = \dfrac{\square}{18} + \dfrac{\square}{18} - \dfrac{\square}{18}$

$=$

(2) $\dfrac{7}{12} - \dfrac{1}{4} + \dfrac{1}{3} =$

(3) $3\dfrac{8}{9} - \dfrac{2}{3} + \dfrac{5}{6} =$

(4) $\dfrac{5}{12} + 2\dfrac{5}{6} - \dfrac{3}{4} =$

(5) $5\dfrac{1}{9} - 4\dfrac{1}{3} + 8\dfrac{2}{5} =$

(6) $6\dfrac{1}{6} - \dfrac{9}{10} + \dfrac{1}{3} =$

(7) $15\dfrac{11}{12} + \dfrac{1}{6} - 8\dfrac{3}{4} =$

(8) $2\dfrac{1}{2} - \dfrac{2}{3} - \dfrac{1}{6} =$

(9) $12\dfrac{1}{9} - \dfrac{1}{3} - \dfrac{1}{2} =$

(10) $4\dfrac{9}{14} - 2\dfrac{6}{7} + 8\dfrac{5}{6} =$

2 Calculate.

5 points per question

(1) $\dfrac{5}{12} - \dfrac{3}{8} + \dfrac{5}{6} =$

(2) $4 - 1\dfrac{2}{3} + \dfrac{1}{4} =$

(3) $5\dfrac{1}{2} - \dfrac{5}{6} + 2\dfrac{2}{3} =$

(4) $6\dfrac{1}{9} + \dfrac{1}{2} - 2\dfrac{2}{3} =$

(5) $\dfrac{1}{12} + 9\dfrac{1}{6} - \dfrac{7}{18} =$

(6) $12\dfrac{6}{7} - 6\dfrac{1}{2} + \dfrac{3}{4} =$

(7) $2\dfrac{2}{3} + \dfrac{3}{4} - 1\dfrac{5}{6} =$

(8) $1\dfrac{2}{3} + 1\dfrac{2}{5} - 1\dfrac{1}{6} =$

(9) $2\dfrac{1}{6} + \dfrac{5}{8} - 1\dfrac{7}{12} =$

(10) $3\dfrac{3}{8} - 1\dfrac{7}{9} + \dfrac{2}{3} =$

You are ready to try this with word problems.

13 Word Problems with Fractions

1 Answer each word problem. Write the question as an expression first, and then calculate.

10 points per question

(1) James pours $\frac{2}{5}$ liter of olive oil from one bottle into another bottle that already has $\frac{1}{10}$ liter of olive oil. How much oil does he have in all?

$$\frac{2}{5} + \frac{1}{10} =$$

⟨Ans.⟩ _____

(2) Sarah used $\frac{1}{9}$ meter of ribbon, and then she used $\frac{1}{3}$ meter more. How much ribbon did she use in all?

⟨Ans.⟩ _____

(3) Otis ran $\frac{1}{2}$ kilometer. His teammate Joris ran $\frac{2}{3}$ kilometer. Then Otis ran another $\frac{1}{6}$ kilometer. How far did they run in all?

$$\frac{1}{2} + \frac{2}{3} + \frac{1}{6} =$$

⟨Ans.⟩ _____

(4) Pat drank $1\frac{1}{3}$ cups of milk. His little sister drank $\frac{1}{2}$ cup of milk. Their dad drank $2\frac{5}{6}$ cups of milk. How much did they drink in all?

⟨Ans.⟩ _____

2 Answer each word problem. Write the question as an expression first, and then calculate. *10 points per question*

(1) Mrs. Rubino had $3\frac{3}{4}$ pounds of cherries. She used $1\frac{2}{5}$ pounds of cherries for a pie. How many pounds of cherries does she have left?

$$3\frac{3}{4} - 1\frac{2}{5} = 3\frac{\square}{20} - 1\frac{\square}{20} =$$

⟨Ans.⟩ _____

(2) There are $2\frac{8}{9}$ cups of flour and $1\frac{1}{3}$ cups of sugar. How much more flour is there than sugar?

⟨Ans.⟩ _____

(3) Juan has $8\frac{4}{15}$ ounces of salt. He uses $5\frac{7}{10}$ ounces for his first science experiment and $1\frac{1}{5}$ ounces for his second experiment. How much salt does he have left?

⟨Ans.⟩ _____

(4) The cafeteria has $15\frac{3}{4}$ gallons of soup. They sell $8\frac{7}{12}$ gallons to students and $2\frac{1}{3}$ gallons to teachers. How much soup is left?

⟨Ans.⟩ _____

3 Answer each word problem. Write the question as an expression first, and then calculate. *10 points per question*

(1) Jennie has $1\frac{7}{15}$ pounds of flour in a bowl. She takes $\frac{4}{5}$ pound out, but then adds $\frac{1}{3}$ pound back in. How many pounds of flour are in the bowl now?

⟨Ans.⟩ _____

(2) Frankie wrote $4\frac{1}{6}$ pages of a story. He didn't like some of it, so he erased $\frac{5}{12}$ page and wrote $\frac{1}{2}$ page more. How many pages long is his story now?

⟨Ans.⟩ _____

Great job! You are ready for the next step.

14 Multiplication of Fractions

1 Multiply.

5 points per question

Example $\dfrac{8}{9} \times \dfrac{1}{3} = \dfrac{8}{27}$

(1) $\dfrac{1}{4} \times \dfrac{1}{3} = \dfrac{\boxed{1}}{12}$

(2) $\dfrac{6}{7} \times \dfrac{3}{5} =$

(3) $\dfrac{4}{9} \times \dfrac{4}{7} =$

(4) $\dfrac{2}{5} \times \dfrac{4}{5} =$

(5) $\dfrac{7}{8} \times \dfrac{3}{4} =$

(6) $\dfrac{4}{7} \times \dfrac{5}{9} =$

(7) $\dfrac{2}{3} \times \dfrac{7}{9} =$

(8) $\dfrac{11}{13} \times \dfrac{1}{2} =$

(9) $\dfrac{11}{12} \times \dfrac{1}{4} =$

(10) $\dfrac{5}{7} \times \dfrac{5}{12} =$

2 Reduce as you multiply.

5 points per question

Example $\dfrac{3}{7} \times \dfrac{4}{9} = \dfrac{\cancel{3}^{1}}{7} \times \dfrac{4}{\cancel{9}_{3}} = \dfrac{4}{21}$

(1) $\dfrac{1}{2} \times \dfrac{4}{5} = \dfrac{1}{\cancel{2}_{1}} \times \dfrac{\cancel{4}^{2}}{5} =$

(2) $\dfrac{10}{11} \times \dfrac{22}{25} = \dfrac{\cancel{10}^{\square}}{\cancel{11}_{\square}} \times \dfrac{\cancel{22}^{\square}}{\cancel{25}_{\square}} = \dfrac{\square}{\square}$

(3) $\dfrac{5}{9} \times \dfrac{4}{15} =$

(4) $\dfrac{7}{11} \times \dfrac{5}{28} =$

(5) $\dfrac{9}{15} \times \dfrac{3}{10} =$

(6) $\dfrac{13}{15} \times \dfrac{25}{26} =$

(7) $\dfrac{15}{17} \times \dfrac{34}{45} =$

(8) $\dfrac{14}{15} \times \dfrac{45}{46} =$

(9) $\dfrac{6}{20} \times \dfrac{5}{22} =$

(10) $\dfrac{9}{10} \times \dfrac{25}{36} =$

Reducing as you multiply will make the problem easier! You won't have to reduce your answer.

Outstanding effort!

15 Multiplication of Fractions

1 Multiply.

5 points per question

Example $\quad 2\dfrac{4}{5} \times 1\dfrac{7}{8} = \dfrac{\cancel{14}^{7}}{5} \times \dfrac{\cancel{15}^{3}}{\cancel{8}_{4}} = \dfrac{21}{4} = 5\dfrac{1}{4}$

Always make your answer a proper fraction.

(1) $1\dfrac{2}{3} \times 2\dfrac{1}{4} = \dfrac{5}{3} \times \dfrac{9}{4} =$

(2) $2\dfrac{1}{4} \times 2\dfrac{2}{13} = \dfrac{9}{4} \times \dfrac{28}{13} =$

(3) $7\dfrac{1}{2} \times 2\dfrac{2}{5} =$

(4) $3\dfrac{3}{7} \times 2\dfrac{7}{12} =$

(5) $4\dfrac{7}{8} \times 1\dfrac{1}{13} =$

(6) $10\dfrac{1}{2} \times 2\dfrac{2}{7} =$

(7) $5\dfrac{5}{6} \times 2\dfrac{2}{5} =$

(8) $4\dfrac{1}{4} \times 2\dfrac{8}{17} =$

(9) $12\dfrac{1}{2} \times 2\dfrac{4}{5} =$

(10) $5\dfrac{4}{7} \times 1\dfrac{8}{13} =$

2 Multiply.

5 points per question

Examples

$$\frac{3}{4} \times \frac{2}{5} \times \frac{5}{11} = \frac{3}{\cancel{4}_2} \times \frac{\cancel{2}^1}{\cancel{5}} \times \frac{\cancel{5}^1}{11} = \frac{3}{22}$$

$$1\frac{1}{2} \times 4\frac{2}{3} \times 2\frac{5}{7} = \frac{3}{\cancel{2}_1} \times \frac{\cancel{14}^{\cancel{7}^1}}{\cancel{3}_1} \times \frac{19}{\cancel{7}_1} = \frac{19}{1} = 19$$

(1) $\frac{3}{4} \times \frac{2}{5} \times \frac{5}{9} =$

(2) $\frac{1}{4} \times \frac{8}{9} \times \frac{3}{5} =$

(3) $1\frac{1}{5} \times \frac{3}{4} \times \frac{8}{9} =$

(4) $5 \times 2\frac{3}{5} \times 1\frac{1}{2} =$

(5) $6 \times 1\frac{2}{3} \times 2\frac{3}{4} =$

(6) $2\frac{1}{4} \times \frac{5}{9} \times 3\frac{2}{5} =$

(7) $\frac{2}{3} \times 5\frac{2}{5} \times 3\frac{3}{4} =$

(8) $\frac{2}{13} \times 1\frac{6}{7} \times 2\frac{4}{5} =$

(9) $12 \times 1\frac{1}{8} \times 1\frac{2}{3} =$

(10) $\frac{4}{11} \times \frac{11}{12} \times 1\frac{3}{10} =$

Your math skills are multiplying!

16 Division of Fractions

1 Divide.

5 points per question

Example $\frac{1}{4} \div \frac{1}{3} = \frac{1}{4} \times \frac{3}{1} = \frac{3}{4}$

When dividing fractions, flip the second fraction and multiply.

(1) $\frac{8}{9} \div \frac{1}{2} = \frac{8}{9} \times \frac{\boxed{2}}{1} =$

(2) $\frac{4}{5} \div \frac{3}{7} = \frac{4}{5} \times \frac{\square}{\square} =$

(3) $\frac{1}{5} \div \frac{4}{9} =$

(4) $\frac{7}{9} \div \frac{2}{5} =$

(5) $\frac{2}{7} \div \frac{5}{8} =$

(6) $\frac{3}{7} \div \frac{5}{6} =$

(7) $\frac{3}{8} \div \frac{2}{7} =$

(8) $\frac{3}{5} \div \frac{7}{9} =$

(9) $\frac{5}{7} \div \frac{2}{9} =$

(10) $\frac{3}{13} \div \frac{1}{12} =$

Don't forget to make your answer a proper fraction.

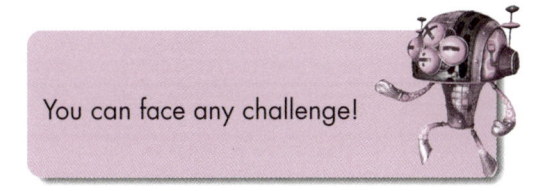

2 Divide.

5 points per question

(1) $\dfrac{6}{7} \div \dfrac{3}{4} = \dfrac{6}{7} \times \dfrac{4}{3} =$

(2) $\dfrac{3}{5} \div \dfrac{9}{10} =$

(3) $\dfrac{5}{6} \div \dfrac{3}{4} =$

(4) $\dfrac{5}{8} \div \dfrac{7}{8} =$

(5) $\dfrac{2}{5} \div \dfrac{14}{15} =$

(6) $\dfrac{3}{8} \div \dfrac{1}{4} =$

(7) $\dfrac{3}{4} \div \dfrac{5}{8} =$

(8) $\dfrac{6}{7} \div \dfrac{4}{5} =$

(9) $\dfrac{7}{8} \div \dfrac{5}{6} =$

(10) $\dfrac{8}{9} \div \dfrac{10}{11} =$

Don't forget to reduce as you compute!

You can face any challenge!

17 Division of Fractions

Level ★★

1 Divide.

5 points per question

(1) $\dfrac{1}{7} \div 4 = \dfrac{1}{7} \div \dfrac{4}{1}$
$= \dfrac{1}{7} \times \dfrac{1}{4}$
$=$

(2) $\dfrac{6}{7} \div 7 = \dfrac{6}{7} \div \dfrac{\Box}{1}$
$=$

(3) $\dfrac{3}{10} \div 4 =$

(4) $5 \div \dfrac{1}{4} = \dfrac{\Box}{1} \div \dfrac{1}{4}$
$=$

(5) $4 \div \dfrac{7}{8} =$

Before dividing, change integers into fractions and change mixed numbers into improper fractions.

2 Divide.

5 points per question

(1) $\dfrac{5}{8} \div \dfrac{3}{4} =$

(2) $\dfrac{4}{9} \div 1\dfrac{5}{6} =$

(3) $1\dfrac{2}{7} \div \dfrac{9}{14} =$

(4) $1\dfrac{5}{9} \div 1\dfrac{1}{6} =$

(5) $2\dfrac{1}{3} \div 1\dfrac{5}{9} =$

Reduce as you compute!

3 Divide.

5 points per question

(1) $\dfrac{2}{3} \div 6 \div \dfrac{3}{4} = \dfrac{2}{3} \div \dfrac{6}{1} \div \dfrac{3}{4}$

$= \dfrac{2}{3} \times \dfrac{1}{6} \times \dfrac{4}{3} =$

(2) $\dfrac{4}{5} \div 1\dfrac{2}{3} \div 1\dfrac{1}{2} = \dfrac{4}{5} \div \dfrac{\Box}{3} \div \dfrac{3}{\Box}$

$=$

(3) $\dfrac{3}{4} \div 5 \div 1\dfrac{1}{5} =$

(4) $\dfrac{7}{24} \div 1\dfrac{7}{8} \div 3\dfrac{1}{2} =$

(5) $6 \div 1\dfrac{2}{3} \div 2\dfrac{4}{5} =$

(6) $11 \div 2\dfrac{2}{3} \div 1\dfrac{4}{7} =$

4 Multiply and divide.

5 points per question

(1) $\dfrac{5}{6} \times \dfrac{3}{4} \div \dfrac{5}{8} = \dfrac{5}{6} \times \dfrac{3}{4} \times \dfrac{8}{5} =$

(2) $\dfrac{7}{8} \div \dfrac{1}{2} \times \dfrac{4}{21} =$

(3) $\dfrac{2}{9} \times \dfrac{6}{7} \div \dfrac{5}{14} =$

(4) $\dfrac{4}{5} \div \dfrac{8}{15} \times 1\dfrac{1}{3} =$

Extra special effort!

18 Word Problems with Fractions

1 Answer each word problem. Write the question as an expression first, and then calculate.

10 points per question

(1) Jacob loves to swim. If he swims $1\frac{1}{4}$ miles every day for 6 days, how far will he have swum in all?

⟨Ans.⟩

(2) The grocer filled 12 bags with cans of food to donate to a local shelter. If each bag weighs $2\frac{4}{9}$ pounds, how much do all the bags weigh together?

⟨Ans.⟩

(3) Jaolen's new toy car can move $4\frac{1}{4}$ feet in $\frac{2}{3}$ second. How far could it go in 6 seconds?

⟨Ans.⟩

(4) A recipe calls for 3 cans of condensed milk. Each can holds $\frac{1}{2}$ cup of condensed milk. If Alice wants to cut the recipe in half, how much condensed milk will she need?

⟨Ans.⟩

2 Answer each word problem.

15 points per question

(1) Jenni loves to crochet. She buys $\frac{5}{7}$ yard of yarn for $2. How much yarn would she get for $1?

$$\frac{5}{7} \div 2 =$$

⟨Ans.⟩ _____

(2) Mrs. Collins teaches pottery. If she divides $\frac{6}{7}$ pound of clay between 3 students, how much clay does each student get?

⟨Ans.⟩ _____

(3) 12 liters of water flow out of the faucet every $\frac{3}{5}$ minute. How much water flows out each minute?

⟨Ans.⟩ _____

(4) The teacher gives each pair of students $1\frac{14}{15}$ liters to water their plants in the garden. If the pairs of students share the water evenly, how much water does each student get?

⟨Ans.⟩ _____

Don't forget to include the units in your answer.

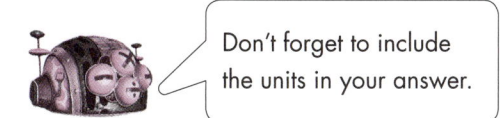

Look as you go!

19 Fraction Review

1 Calculate.
5 points per question

(1) $\dfrac{5}{7} + \dfrac{4}{5} =$

(2) $1\dfrac{3}{10} + 2\dfrac{1}{7} + \dfrac{2}{5} =$

(3) $5\dfrac{1}{3} - 2\dfrac{3}{7} =$

(4) $2\dfrac{11}{14} - 1\dfrac{1}{7} - \dfrac{1}{2} =$

(5) $5\dfrac{3}{4} - 2\dfrac{7}{12} + 1\dfrac{1}{3} =$

(6) $5\dfrac{1}{9} - 4\dfrac{1}{3} + 2\dfrac{2}{5} =$

2 Calculate.
5 points per question

(1) $3\dfrac{3}{7} \times 2\dfrac{7}{12} =$

(2) $6 \times 1\dfrac{1}{4} \times 1\dfrac{2}{3} =$

(3) $1\dfrac{2}{7} \div 1\dfrac{9}{14} =$

(4) $1\dfrac{5}{6} \div \dfrac{1}{2} \div 12 =$

(5) $11 \times 2\dfrac{2}{3} \div 1\dfrac{4}{7} =$

(6) $\dfrac{7}{24} \times 1\dfrac{7}{8} \div 3\dfrac{1}{2} =$

3 Answer each word problem. Write the question as an expression first, and then calculate.   10 points per question

(1) A meatloaf recipe calls for $1\frac{3}{4}$ pounds of ground beef, $1\frac{1}{3}$ pounds of onions, and $1\frac{1}{6}$ pounds of ground sausage. How much do these ingredients weigh in all?

⟨Ans.⟩ _____

(2) Juliette adds $5\frac{1}{9}$ cups of nuts to $1\frac{1}{3}$ cups of pretzels. She puts $1\frac{5}{18}$ cups of the trail mix in her cupboard and takes the rest to a party. How much trail mix does she take to the party?

⟨Ans.⟩ _____

4 Answer each word problem. Write the question as an expression first, and then calculate.   10 points per question

(1) Sophie jogs $4\frac{1}{4}$ miles in $\frac{7}{8}$ hour. How far would she run in $4\frac{1}{2}$ hours if she kept the same pace?

⟨Ans.⟩ _____

(2) Lana's toy boat can sail $7\frac{1}{2}$ yards in $4\frac{1}{6}$ minutes. How far would it sail in $8\frac{3}{4}$ minutes if it kept the same pace?

⟨Ans.⟩ _____

You've got it!

20 Place Value Review

Don't forget!

Whole numbers like 0, 1, 2, and 3 are called **integers**.

Numbers like 0.1, 0.5, and 2.3 are called **decimals**, and the "." is called the **decimal point**.

The places to the right of the decimal point are called **tenths, hundredths, thousandths**, and so on.

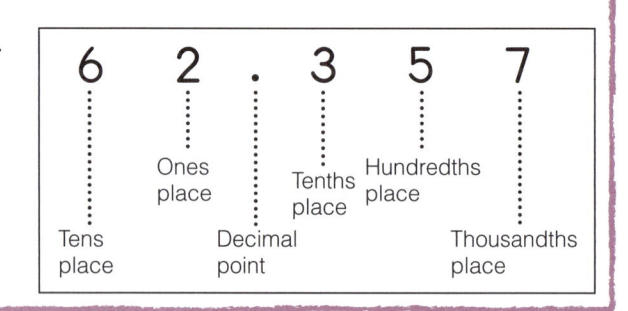

```
6   2 . 3   5   7
|   |   |   |   |
Tens Ones Decimal Tenths Hundredths Thousandths
place place point place place place
```

1 Write the appropriate number in each box.
4 points per question

(1) The number in the ones place of 4.63 is ☐ and in the tenths place is ☐.

(2) The number in the tenths place of 6.24 is ☐ and in the hundredths place is ☐.

(3) The number in the ones place of 8.712 is ☐ and in the thousandths place is ☐.

(4) The number in the tenths place of 42.903 is ☐ and in the thousandths place is ☐.

(5) The number in the tens place of 76.42 is ☐ and in the tenths place is ☐.

2 Write the appropriate number in each box.
5 points per question

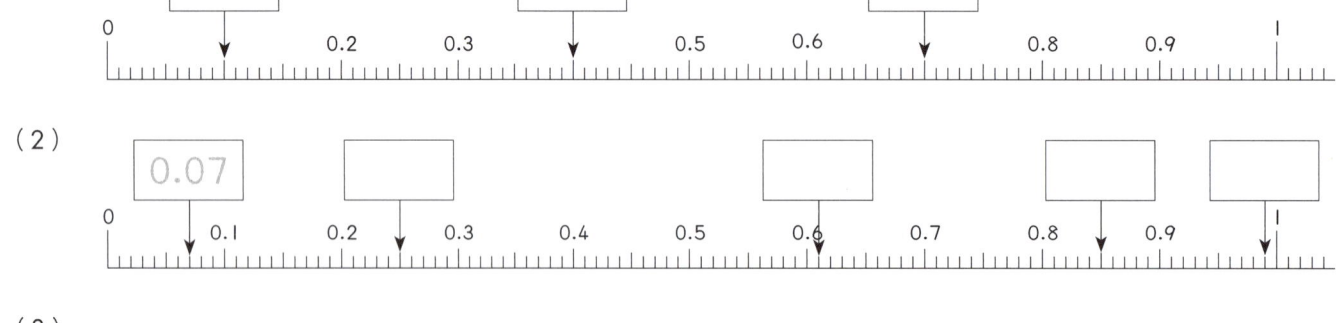

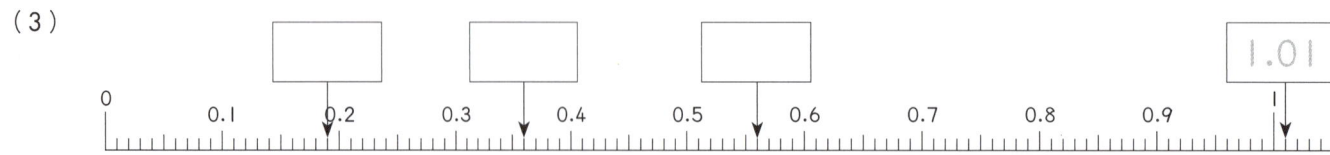

(1) Number line from 0 to 1: 0.1 shown; blanks at 0.4 and 0.7.

(2) Number line from 0 to 1 (hundredths): 0.07 shown; blanks at 0.17, 0.57, 0.87, 0.97.

(3) Number line from 0 to just past 1: 1.01 shown; blanks at 0.21, 0.41, 0.61.

40 © Kumon Publishing Co., Ltd.

Don't forget!

A **round number** is made by adjusting a number up or down in order to simplify the number for easier calculations. If the number in the next place is 5 or higher, round up. If it is 4 or lower, round down.

Example
Round to the nearest tenths place.
4.6⑦24 → 4.7
(round up)

Example
Round to the nearest thousandths place.
76.492③2 → 76.492
(round down)

3 Round each number to the nearest tenths place. — 5 points per question

(1) 6.72 ( )   (2) 8.473 ( )   (3) 0.1574 ( )

4 Round each number to the nearest hundredths place. — 5 points per question

(1) 8.921 ( )   (2) 4.445 ( )   (3) 0.1119 ( )

5 Round each number to the nearest thousandths place. — 5 points per question

(1) 0.1574 ( )   (2) 0.1119 ( )   (3) 23.78263 ( )

6 A scientist is measuring the wing size of bees. Round each length to the nearest thousandths place. — 5 points per question

(1) Bee A's wings measured
0.0146 m   ( ) m

(2) Bee B's wings measured
0.0152 m   ( ) m

(3) Bee C's wings measured
0.0137 m   ( ) m

(4) Bee D's wings measured
0.0163 m   ( ) m

Well done!

21 Decimals as Fractions

1 Rewrite each decimal as a fraction. Then reduce.

4 points per question

Examples

$0.2 = \dfrac{2}{10} = \dfrac{1}{5}$ Tenths place

$0.02 = \dfrac{2}{100} = \dfrac{1}{50}$ Hundredths place

$0.002 = \dfrac{2}{1000} = \dfrac{1}{500}$ Thousandths place

(1) $0.5 = \dfrac{\Box}{\Box} = \dfrac{\Box}{\Box}$

(2) $0.8 = \dfrac{\Box}{\Box} = \dfrac{\Box}{\Box}$

(3) $0.25 = \dfrac{\Box}{\Box} = \dfrac{\Box}{\Box}$

(4) $0.35 = \dfrac{\Box}{\Box} = \dfrac{\Box}{\Box}$

(5) $0.05 = \dfrac{\Box}{\Box} = \dfrac{\Box}{\Box}$

(6) $0.18 = \dfrac{\Box}{\Box} = \dfrac{\Box}{\Box}$

(7) $0.08 = \dfrac{\Box}{\Box} = \dfrac{\Box}{\Box}$

(8) $0.005 = \dfrac{\Box}{\Box} = \dfrac{\Box}{\Box}$

(9) $0.825 = \dfrac{\Box}{\Box} = \dfrac{\Box}{\Box}$

(10) $0.404 = \dfrac{\Box}{\Box} = \dfrac{\Box}{\Box}$

2 Rewrite each decimal as a mixed number. Then reduce.   5 points per question

Examples

$1.4 = 1\frac{4}{10} = 1\frac{2}{5}$ $1.04 = 1\frac{4}{100} = 1\frac{1}{25}$ $1.004 = 1\frac{4}{1000} = 1\frac{1}{250}$

(1) $3.5 =$

(2) $5.75 =$

(3) $2.6 =$

(4) $2.68 =$

(5) $10.55 =$

(6) $9.005 =$

3 Rewrite each decimal as an improper fraction. Then reduce.   5 points per question

Example $3.2 = \frac{32}{10} = \frac{16}{5}$

(1) $2.5 =$

(2) $3.4 =$

(3) $1.12 =$

(4) $2.08 =$

(5) $1.625 =$

(6) $2.008 =$

You can do anything with decimals!

22 Fractions as Decimals

1 Rewrite each fraction as a decimal.

5 points per question

Examples

$\frac{2}{5} \longrightarrow 5\overline{)2.0}$ gives 0.4

$\frac{2}{5} = 0.4$

$\frac{8}{5} \longrightarrow 5\overline{)8.0}$ gives 1.6

$\frac{8}{5} = 1.6$

(1) $\frac{1}{4} =$

(2) $\frac{3}{4} =$

(3) $\frac{4}{5} =$

(4) $\frac{7}{5} =$

(5) $\frac{3}{50} =$

(6) $\frac{3}{8} =$

(7) $\frac{33}{4} =$

(8) $\frac{31}{4} =$

2 Rewrite each mixed fraction as a decimal.

6 points per question

Example

$1\dfrac{3}{5} = 1.6$

```
   0.6
5)3.0
   3 0
   ───
     0
```

(1) $2\dfrac{1}{4} =$

(2) $7\dfrac{4}{5} =$

(3) $5\dfrac{3}{8} =$

(4) $4\dfrac{3}{25} =$

(5) $3\dfrac{31}{50} =$

(6) $10\dfrac{1}{5} =$

(7) $5\dfrac{12}{25} =$

(8) $2\dfrac{21}{35} =$

(9) $7\dfrac{7}{8} =$

(10) $2\dfrac{5}{8} =$

You did so well!

23 Percents

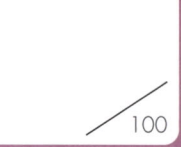

1 Rewrite each decimal as a fraction and a percent.

5 points per question

Examples

$0.02 = \dfrac{2}{100} = 2\%$ (Hundredths place)

$0.20 = \dfrac{20}{100} = 20\%$ (Hundredths place)

$2.00 = \dfrac{200}{100} = 200\%$ (Hundredths place)

(1) $0.45 = \dfrac{\square}{100} =$

(2) $0.35 = \dfrac{}{100} =$

(3) $0.4 = \dfrac{}{100} =$

(4) $0.04 = \dfrac{}{100} =$

(5) $0.004 = \dfrac{4}{1000} = 0.4\%$

(6) $0.123 = \dfrac{123}{1000} = 12.3\%$

(7) $0.971 = \dfrac{}{1000} =$

(8) $0.979 = \dfrac{}{1000} =$

(9) $0.4805 = \dfrac{}{10000} =$

(10) $0.0003 = \dfrac{}{10000} =$

Move the decimal point two places to the right to quickly change a decimal to a percent.

2 Rewrite each integer as a percent.

5 points per question

(1) 1 = 100 %

(2) 1.45 =

(3) 1.04 =

(4) 1.045 =

(5) 10.47 =

(6) 1.005 = 100.5 %

(7) 1.012 =

(8) 1.103 =

(9) 2 =

(10) 2.02 =

You get 100% for effort.

24 Percents

Date / / **Name**

Level ★★★ Score /100

1 Rewrite each percent as a fraction and a decimal.

5 points per question

(1) $45\% = \dfrac{\square}{100} =$

(2) $55\% = \dfrac{\square}{100} =$

(3) $70\% = \dfrac{\square}{\square} =$

(4) $87\% = \dfrac{\square}{\square} =$

(5) $6\% = \dfrac{\square}{\square} =$

(6) $26.4\% = \dfrac{\square}{\square} =$

(7) $14.9\% = \dfrac{\square}{\square} =$

(8) $0.8\% = \dfrac{\square}{1000} =$

(9) $67.02\% = \dfrac{\square}{\square} =$

(10) $0.09\% = \dfrac{\square}{\square} =$

Move the decimal point two places to the left to quickly change a percent into a decimal.

48 © Kumon Publishing Co., Ltd.

2 Rewrite each percent as an integer.

5 points per question

(1) 100 % =

(2) 145 % =

(3) 108 % =

(4) 117 % =

(5) 110 % =

(6) 1,000 % =

(7) 1,100 % =

(8) 1,110 % =

(9) 1,111 % =

(10) 1,011 % =

Percents are challenging, but you can do it!

25 Percents

Date / /   Name

Level ★★★   Score /100

1 Rewrite each percent as a decimal and a fraction. Then reduce each fraction.   4 points per question

(1) 25% = 0.25 = $\frac{25}{100}$ = $\frac{1}{4}$

(2) 75% =

(3) 60% =

(4) 15% =

(5) 26% =

(6) 150% =

(7) 125% =

(8) 105% =

(9) 10.5% =

(10) 100.5% =

2 Rewrite each fraction as a decimal and a percent.   5 points per question

(1) $\frac{1}{2}$ = 0.5 = 50%

(2) $\frac{1}{4}$ =   =

(3) $\frac{2}{5}$ =   =

(4) $\frac{7}{20}$ =   =

(5) $1\frac{4}{5}$ =   =

(6) $1\frac{3}{4}$ =   =

3 Answer each word problem.   5 points per question

(1) Aunt Miriam buys a pen for $0.82. What percent of a dollar was spent on the pen?

⟨Ans.⟩ _____

(2) In Teaneck Village, it rained 1.47 times the usual amount during the season. What percentage of the usual amount of rain did the village receive?

⟨Ans.⟩ _____

4 Answer each word problem.   5 points per question

(1) Yen sells ice cream. His sales increased by 8,250 % since winter. Represent his sales increase as an integer.

⟨Ans.⟩ _____

(2) Lana adds some tomato plants to her vegetable garden. This increases the size of her garden by 27 %. Represent the size of growth as an integer.

⟨Ans.⟩ _____

5 Answer each word problem.   5 points per question

(1) Derik pumps gas into his truck so it is $\frac{5}{8}$ full. What percent of his gas tank is full?

⟨Ans.⟩ _____

(2) A jar of jelly beans is $\frac{1}{5}$ full. What percent of the jar is full?

⟨Ans.⟩ _____

You've mastered percents!

26 Decimals and Fractions

1 Calculate.

5 points per question

Convert each decimal into a fraction first to calculate.

(1) $\dfrac{1}{6} + 0.5 =$

(2) $0.45 + \dfrac{1}{5} =$

(3) $0.85 + \dfrac{3}{5} =$

(4) $1\dfrac{5}{6} + 0.5 =$

(5) $1\dfrac{1}{8} + 0.6 =$

(6) $0.75 - \dfrac{1}{3} =$

(7) $\dfrac{17}{20} - 0.55 =$

(8) $\dfrac{7}{12} - 0.35 =$

(9) $2.75 - \dfrac{2}{3} =$

(10) $4\dfrac{7}{10} - 1.35 =$

2 Calculate.

5 points per question

(1) $\frac{1}{4} + 0.25 + \frac{2}{5} =$

(2) $\frac{5}{6} + 0.4 + \frac{2}{3} =$

(3) $0.25 + \frac{1}{8} + 0.6 =$

(4) $6\frac{17}{20} - 1.4 - \frac{3}{10} =$

(5) $7\frac{1}{4} - 1.2 - 3\frac{1}{5} =$

(6) $5\frac{9}{10} - 2.3 - 1\frac{13}{20} =$

(7) $\frac{9}{10} + 0.45 - \frac{11}{20} =$

(8) $\frac{5}{6} - 0.25 + \frac{3}{8} =$

(9) $0.875 - \frac{3}{4} + 1\frac{2}{3} =$

(10) $0.75 + \frac{4}{9} - \frac{5}{6} =$

Fantastic work!

27 Decimals and Fractions

1 Calculate.

5 points per question

(1) $\dfrac{1}{6} \times 0.5 =$

(2) $\dfrac{5}{6} \times 0.75 =$

(3) $\dfrac{5}{12} \times 0.08 =$

(4) $2\dfrac{2}{3} \times 0.9 =$

(5) $0.04 \times 1\dfrac{2}{3} =$

(6) $0.45 \div \dfrac{1}{4} =$

(7) $0.55 \div \dfrac{9}{10} =$

(8) $0.325 \div \dfrac{1}{6} =$

(9) $1\dfrac{1}{12} \div 0.13 =$

(10) $0.625 \div 2\dfrac{1}{12} =$

Reduce as you multiply.

Convert each decimal into a fraction to calculate.

2 Calculate.

5 points per question

(1) $\dfrac{5}{6} \times \dfrac{2}{3} \times 0.9 =$

(2) $\dfrac{5}{8} \div \dfrac{8}{9} \times 0.8 =$

(3) $\dfrac{5}{7} \times 0.4 \div \dfrac{3}{7} =$

(4) $0.6 \times \dfrac{2}{3} \div 0.42 =$

(5) $\dfrac{5}{7} \times 0.25 \div \dfrac{2}{7} =$

(6) $\dfrac{3}{4} \div \dfrac{2}{3} \div 0.2 =$

(7) $1.8 \div \dfrac{5}{8} \times \dfrac{8}{9} =$

(8) $2\dfrac{5}{7} \times 1.4 \div 1\dfrac{3}{7} =$

(9) $2\dfrac{1}{3} \times 4 \times 1.2 =$

(10) $1\dfrac{5}{12} \div 1.25 \div 1\dfrac{2}{3} =$

28 Word Problems with Decimals and Fractions

1 Answer each word problem. Write the question as an expression first, and then calculate.   10 points per question

(1) Spencer pours 0.15 liter of water out of a full jug that holds $\frac{9}{10}$ liter. Then he adds $\frac{3}{100}$ liter back. How much water is in the jug?

⟨Ans.⟩ _____

(2) Sheila knits $6\frac{9}{10}$ feet of a blanket. She unravels 2.15 feet off of it and knits $\frac{1}{6}$ foot back onto it. How long is the blanket?

⟨Ans.⟩ _____

2 Answer each word problem. Write the question as an expression first, and then calculate.   10 points per question

(1) Christopher has 4.5 pieces of wood. Each full piece is $1\frac{8}{15}$ yards long. How long is the wood if Christopher glues the pieces together?

⟨Ans.⟩ _____

(2) Gene has $3\frac{1}{3}$ pieces of ribbon. Each full piece is 2.15 meters long. How long is the ribbon if Gene glues the pieces together?

⟨Ans.⟩ _____

3 Answer each word problem. Write the question as an expression first, and then calculate.   15 points per question

(1) Matthew has $3\frac{1}{3}$ pieces of copper pipe. Each full piece is 2.5 meters long. If Matthew welds the pieces together and then divides the new pipe into $\frac{5}{6}$ meter pieces, how many pieces will he have?

⟨Ans.⟩ _____

(2) Dominic has 6.75 pieces of wood. Each full piece is 1.2 yards long. If he glues the pieces together and then cuts the new wood every $\frac{9}{10}$ yards, how many pieces of wood will he have?

⟨Ans.⟩ _____

4 Answer each word problem. Write the question as an expression first, and then calculate.   15 points per question

(1) A baker uses 0.6 ton of whole wheat flour each month. $\frac{1}{9}$ of the whole wheat flour is used for muffins. If the baker adds 0.1 ton of all-purpose flour to the muffin mix, how much does the muffin mix weigh?

⟨Ans.⟩ _____

(2) A scientist has a 1.5 liter bottle of water. He pours $\frac{9}{10}$ of the bottle into a beaker and boils it so 0.25 liter of the liquid evaporates. How much water is left in the beaker?

⟨Ans.⟩ _____

You can work through anything!

29 Exponents

1 Calculate.

5 points per question

Examples

$4^2 = 4 \times 4 = 16$ — 4^2 is read as "four squared."
$4^3 = 4 \times 4 \times 4 = 64$ — 4^3 is read as "four cubed."

(1) $2^2 = 2 \times 2 =$

(2) $2^3 = 2 \times 2 \times 2 =$

(3) $2^4 = 2 \times 2 \times 2 \times 2 =$

(4) $3^2 =$

(5) $3^3 =$

(6) $3^0 =$

(7) $3^5 =$

(8) $4^4 =$

(9) $6^0 =$

(10) $7^3 =$

Any number raised to the power of 0 equals 1.

3^4 can be read as "three to the fourth power." 3^5 can be read as "three to the fifth power."

2 Calculate.

5 points per question

Examples $\left(\dfrac{2}{3}\right)^2 = \dfrac{2}{3} \times \dfrac{2}{3} = \dfrac{4}{9}$ $\dfrac{2}{3^2} \times \dfrac{2}{3 \times 3} = \dfrac{2}{9}$

(1) $\left(\dfrac{1}{2}\right)^2 = \dfrac{1}{2} \times \dfrac{1}{2} =$

(2) $\left(\dfrac{1}{2}\right)^3 =$

(3) $\left(\dfrac{1}{4}\right)^2 =$

(4) $\dfrac{1}{4^2} = \dfrac{1}{4 \times 4} =$

(5) $\dfrac{3}{5^3} =$

(6) $\left(\dfrac{3}{5}\right)^0 =$

3 Answer each word problem.

10 points per question

(1) The volume of a cube can be calculated by multiplying the width, length, and height, which are all equal lengths. If the width, length, and height of Sunny's block each equal $\dfrac{3}{4}$ inch, what is the volume of the block?

$\left(\dfrac{3}{4}\right)^3 =$

⟨Ans.⟩ _____ in³

(2) The cafeteria cook wants to find out the volume of a cube cooler he will fill with ice. If one side of the cube is $\dfrac{4}{5}$ foot, what is the volume of the cooler?

$\left(\dfrac{4}{5}\right)^3 =$

⟨Ans.⟩ _____ ft³

You've got the power!

30 Exponents

1 Calculate.

4 points per question

(1) $\left(1\dfrac{1}{3}\right)^2 = \left(\dfrac{4}{3}\right)^2 =$

(2) $\left(1\dfrac{1}{3}\right)^3 =$

(3) $\left(1\dfrac{1}{2}\right)^3 =$

(4) $\left(1\dfrac{1}{2}\right)^4 =$

(5) $\left(2\dfrac{1}{2}\right)^2 =$

(6) $\left(1\dfrac{2}{3}\right)^2 =$

(7) $\left(2\dfrac{1}{4}\right)^2 =$

(8) $\left(1\dfrac{2}{3}\right)^3 =$

(9) $\left(2\dfrac{1}{4}\right)^0 =$

(10) $\left(3\dfrac{3}{4}\right)^2 =$

Convert mixed numbers to improper fractions before calculating.

Don't forget that any number raised to the power of 0 equals 1.

2 Calculate.   5 points per question

(1) $2^5 \times \dfrac{1}{2^2} = 2 \times 2 \times 2 \times 2 \times 2 \times \dfrac{1}{2 \times 2}$

$=$

(2) $3^4 \times \left(\dfrac{1}{6}\right)^3 = 3 \times 3 \times 3 \times 3 \times \dfrac{1}{6 \times 6 \times 6}$

$=$

(3) $4^3 \times \left(\dfrac{1}{4}\right)^2 =$

(4) $5^4 \times \dfrac{1}{10^3} =$

(5) $8^2 \times \dfrac{3}{4^2} =$

(6) $9^3 \times \left(\dfrac{2}{3}\right)^4 =$

3 Calculate.   5 points per question

(1) $\left(1\dfrac{1}{3}\right)^2 \times \left(\dfrac{3}{4}\right)^3 = \left(\dfrac{4}{3}\right)^2 \times \left(\dfrac{3}{4}\right)^3$

$= \dfrac{4}{3} \times \dfrac{4}{3} \times \dfrac{3}{4} \times \dfrac{3}{4} \times \dfrac{3}{4} =$

(2) $\left(1\dfrac{1}{2}\right)^3 \times 6^2 =$

(3) $8^2 \times \left(2\dfrac{1}{2}\right)^4 =$

(4) $9^2 \times \left(1\dfrac{1}{3}\right)^4 =$

(5) $\left(2\dfrac{1}{2}\right)^4 \times \left(2\dfrac{2}{5}\right)^2 =$

(6) $\left(1\dfrac{1}{4}\right)^2 \times \dfrac{2}{3^3} =$

Convert mixed numbers to improper fractions before calculating.

Amazing work!

31 Order of Operations

1 Calculate. Write the intermediate steps taken to calculate each answer. 5 points per question

Don't forget!

According to the order of operations,
- **calculate the numbers in parentheses first**
- then calculate from left to right

Example 6 − (7 − 2) = 6 − 5 = 1

(1) 7 − (8 − 3) = 7 − ☐ =

(2) 8 − (9 − 5) =

(3) 8 + (10 − 9) =

(4) (5 − 2) + 6 =

(5) (8 − 5) + 4 =

(6) (10 − 2) × 7 = 8 × 7 =

(7) 4 × (2 − 1) =

(8) 2 × (8 − 5) =

(9) (15 − 7) ÷ 2 =

(10) 18 ÷ (8 − 5) =

62 © Kumon Publishing Co., Ltd.

2 **Calculate. Write the intermediate steps.**   5 points per question

(1) $\dfrac{5}{7} - \left(\dfrac{6}{7} - \dfrac{2}{7}\right) = \dfrac{5}{7} - \dfrac{\square}{7} =$

(2) $\dfrac{1}{2} + \left(5 - \dfrac{1}{4}\right) = \dfrac{1}{2} + \left(\dfrac{\square}{4} - \dfrac{1}{4}\right)$

$=$

(3) $4 \times \left(\dfrac{5}{6} - \dfrac{2}{3}\right) =$

(4) $\left(\dfrac{4}{5} - \dfrac{2}{3}\right) \div \dfrac{1}{3} =$

(5) $(10 - 2) + (13 - 6) =$

(6) $(6 - 4) + \left(1\dfrac{5}{6} - 1\dfrac{2}{3}\right) =$

(7) $4 \times (7 \div 2) = \overset{2}{4} \times \dfrac{7}{2} =$

(8) $(9 \div 4) \times \dfrac{1}{3} =$

(9) $(7 - 3) \times \left(\dfrac{1}{2} + \dfrac{1}{4}\right) =$

(10) $\left(\dfrac{4}{5} + \dfrac{2}{3}\right) \div \left(\dfrac{3}{5} - \dfrac{1}{3}\right) =$

You thought this through!

32 Order of Operations

1 Calculate. Write the intermediate steps.

5 points per question

Don't forget!
According to the order of operations,
- **calculate the numbers in parentheses and brackets first (start with the innermost and continue to the outermost)**
- then calculate from left to right

Example $8-[9-(2+3)]=8-[9-5]=8-4=4$

(1) $[4+(8-1)]-9=[4+\square]-9$
$=\square-9$
$=$

(2) $[12-(15-7)]+3=$

(3) $20-[(4+8)-1]=$

(4) $2\times[9-(6-3)]=$

(5) $7\div[2+(6-2)]=$

(6) $[3\div(2-1)]+\dfrac{5}{7}=[\square\div\square]+\dfrac{5}{7}$
$=\square+\dfrac{5}{7}$
$=3\dfrac{5}{7}$

(7) $9\times\left[\dfrac{1}{6}+\left(\dfrac{1}{2}-\dfrac{1}{3}\right)\right]=$

(8) $\left[\dfrac{3}{4}+\left(2-\dfrac{1}{2}\right)\right]+1\dfrac{5}{7}=$

(9) $\left[\left(\dfrac{1}{5}+1\dfrac{1}{10}\right)-\dfrac{1}{2}\right]\div\dfrac{1}{5}=$

(10) $\left[(10-8)-1\dfrac{6}{7}\right]+\left[9-\left(4-\dfrac{5}{7}\right)\right]$
$=$

2 Calculate. Write the intermediate steps.

5 points per question

(1) $6 - \left[\left(\dfrac{1}{4} + 0.75\right) - \dfrac{3}{4}\right]$

$= 6 - \left[\left(\dfrac{1}{4} + \dfrac{\square}{\square}\right) - \dfrac{3}{4}\right] =$

(2) $4 - \left[\dfrac{1}{3} + \left(1.5 - 0.4\right)\right]$

$= 4 - \left[\dfrac{1}{3} + 1.1\right] = 4 - \left[\dfrac{1}{3} + 1\dfrac{\square}{\square}\right]$

$=$

(3) $\left[2.6 + \left(2 \times \dfrac{1}{2}\right)\right] - 2.8$

$=$

(4) $\left[3 \times \left(1.75 - \dfrac{3}{4}\right)\right] + 3.5$

$=$

(5) $2 \times \left[1\dfrac{1}{2} + (3.3 - 1.1)\right]$

$=$

(6) $\left[5\dfrac{5}{6} - \left(2.5 - \dfrac{2}{3}\right)\right] \div \dfrac{2}{3}$

$=$

(7) $0.5 \times \left[16 \times \left(2 - 1\dfrac{1}{4}\right)\right]$

$=$

(8) $17 \div \left[0.4 + \left(1\dfrac{5}{6} - 1\dfrac{2}{3}\right)\right]$

$=$

(9) $\dfrac{5}{6} \times \left[3 \div \left(0.625 - \dfrac{3}{8}\right)\right]$

$=$

(10) $5.4 + \left[2 + \left(1\dfrac{1}{4} \div \dfrac{3}{4}\right)\right]$

$=$

Convert decimals to fractions if necessary to calculate.

Nicely done!

Order of Operations

33

1 Calculate. Write the intermediate steps.

5 points per question

Don't forget!

According to the order of operations,
- calculate exponents and numbers in parentheses and brackets first (start with the innermost and continue to the outermost)
- then calculate from left to right

Example $(5-2)^3 \times \dfrac{1}{9} = 3^3 \times \dfrac{1}{9} = \overset{3}{\underset{1}{27}} \times \dfrac{1}{9} = 3$

(1) $3^2 - [4 + (2+3)] = 3^2 - [4 + \boxed{}]$

$= 3^2 - \boxed{} = \boxed{} - \boxed{} =$

(2) $(18 \div 9)^3 \times (3+1) =$

(3) $[(4+5) + 3^2] + 3^0 =$

(4) $[15 - (7+6)]^3 - (4+2)$

$=$

(5) $[2 + (3^2 - 4)] \times \dfrac{5}{7}$

$= [2 + (\boxed{} - 4)] \times \dfrac{5}{7}$

$= [2 + \boxed{}] \times \dfrac{5}{7} =$

(6) $7 \div \left[3^2 - \left(\dfrac{1}{2} + \dfrac{1}{3}\right)\right]$

$= 7 \div \left[3^2 - \left(\dfrac{3}{6} + \dfrac{2}{6}\right)\right] =$

(7) $3^2 - \left[\dfrac{1}{4^2} + \left(\dfrac{1}{2} + \dfrac{1}{4}\right)\right] =$

(8) $\left[\left(\dfrac{1}{4^2} + \dfrac{9}{2^4}\right) \div \dfrac{1}{2^2}\right] + 1 =$

2 Calculate. Write the intermediate steps.

6 points per question

(1) $4^2 + \left[\dfrac{1}{6^2} + \left(\dfrac{1}{2} - \dfrac{1}{4}\right)\right]$

=

(2) $\left(\dfrac{5}{7}\right)^2 + [10 + (8-7)^5]$

=

(3) $\left[\left(\dfrac{1}{2}\right)^3 + \left(\dfrac{1}{4}\right)^2\right] \times 4^2$

=

(4) $2^3 \times \left[\left(\dfrac{1}{3}\right)^2 - \left(\dfrac{1}{6}\right)^2\right]$

=

(5) $\left[\dfrac{3}{4} - \left(\dfrac{2}{3}\right)^2\right] \times \left(\dfrac{2}{3}\right)^2$

=

(6) $\left[\left(2\dfrac{2}{3}\right)^2 - \dfrac{8}{9}\right] - \dfrac{2}{3^2}$

=

(7) $\dfrac{2^2}{5} + \left[2^3 - \left(1\dfrac{1}{2}\right)^2\right]$

=

(8) $\left[2\dfrac{1}{10} - \left(1\dfrac{1}{5}\right)^2 + 2^2\right] \div \left(\dfrac{3}{10}\right)^2$

=

(9) $[12 - (5-3)^3] + \left[\left(1\dfrac{1}{8}\right)^2 - \dfrac{1}{2^3}\right]$

=

(10) $\left[\dfrac{8}{9} \div \left(\dfrac{8}{9} - \dfrac{2}{3}\right)^2\right] \times \left(1\dfrac{1}{3}\right)^2$

=

These are tough, but you can do it!

34 Order of Operations

1 Calculate. Write the intermediate steps.

5 points per question

(1) $3^2 - \left(0.5 + \dfrac{1}{4}\right) =$

(2) $2^4 - \left(\dfrac{2}{3} + 0.75\right) =$

(3) $0.25 + 2^3 - \dfrac{1}{2^2} =$

(4) $4^2 + \left(0.75 - \dfrac{1}{3^2}\right) =$

(5) $\left[7 \div \left(0.25 \times \dfrac{4}{5}\right)\right] - 5^2$
=

(6) $\left[4^2 \times \left(0.1 + \dfrac{2}{5}\right)\right] + 1\dfrac{3}{5}$
=

(7) $10^2 \div \left[0.2 \div \left(\dfrac{1}{5}\right)^2\right] + 2^4$
=

(8) $\left[2.6 + \left(\dfrac{7}{15} - \dfrac{2}{5}\right)\right] \div \dfrac{1}{3}$
=

Convert decimals to fractions whenever necessary.

2 Calculate. Write the intermediate steps.

10 points per question

(1) $\left[\left(1\frac{1}{4}+0.25\right)\times 2^2\right]\div\frac{1}{3}$

=

(2) $\left[\left(1\frac{2}{3}+1.75\right)\times 3\right]-\frac{1}{2^2}$

=

(3) $\left[\left(\frac{2}{3}+4.125\right)+\left(\frac{1}{2}\right)^2\right]+2^3$

=

(4) $\frac{2}{4^2}\times\left[\left(1.5\times 2\frac{1}{3}\right)\div\frac{7}{8}\right]^2$

=

(5) $\left(1.375+\frac{9}{2^3}\right)+(18-4^2)^2+2\frac{5}{8}$

=

(6) $\left(2.6-1\frac{3}{5}\right)^2+3^3-\left(4.2-3\frac{1}{5}\right)^3$

=

Calculate from inside to outside and left to right.

Wow! You made it!

35 Order of Operations

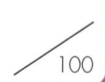

1 Calculate. Write the intermediate steps.   5 points per question

Don't forget!
According to the order of operations,
- calculate exponents and numbers in parentheses and brackets first
- **perform multiplication and division before addition and subtraction**
- then calculate from left to right

Examples $2+6\times3=2+18=20$ $12\div4-1=3-1=2$

(1) $6-8\div2=6-\boxed{}=$

(2) $4+3\times2=$

(3) $20-18\div2=$

(4) $\dfrac{2}{3}+2\div3=\dfrac{2}{3}+\dfrac{\boxed{}}{\boxed{}}=$

(5) $8-\dfrac{2}{7}\times\dfrac{7}{8}=$

(6) $3\dfrac{1}{2}-3\div2=$

(7) $11\div2+4\dfrac{1}{2}=$

(8) $6+2\times1\dfrac{3}{4}=$

(9) $2\dfrac{2}{3}-4\div9=$

(10) $\dfrac{5}{6}-\dfrac{1}{3}\div\dfrac{1}{2}+1=$

2 Calculate. Write the intermediate steps.

5 points per question

(1) $1\dfrac{3}{8} \times 2 - 1\dfrac{1}{4} =$

(2) $3\dfrac{1}{4} - 2\dfrac{1}{3} \times \dfrac{3}{4} =$

(3) $2\dfrac{1}{5} - \dfrac{2}{3} \times \dfrac{3}{4} =$

(4) $4\dfrac{1}{6} - 2\dfrac{2}{3} \div 3\dfrac{1}{5} =$

(5) $6\dfrac{1}{2} + 3\dfrac{2}{5} \times \dfrac{5}{6} =$

(6) $2\dfrac{2}{5} \div 1\dfrac{7}{17} - \dfrac{11}{15} =$

(7) $3\dfrac{3}{4} \times \dfrac{2}{3} - 1\dfrac{3}{4} =$

(8) $3 - 2\dfrac{1}{4} \div 2\dfrac{5}{8} =$

(9) $2 + 1\dfrac{2}{5} \times 3\dfrac{4}{7} =$

(10) $1\dfrac{5}{9} \div 2\dfrac{1}{3} - \dfrac{1}{6} =$

Outstanding effort!

36 Word Problems with Order of Operations

Level ★★★

1 Answer each word problem. Write the question as an expression first, and then calculate. — 10 points per question

(1) Ricardo baked 15 cupcakes for a party. 16 guests were invited, but 3 people didn't come. If each attending guest had a cupcake, how many cupcakes were left over?

☐ − (☐ − ☐) =

⟨Ans.⟩ _____

(2) Matilda promised to make a bracelet for each of her 9 friends. She made the same promise to her 5 cousins. If she makes 8 bracelets on Saturday and 8 more on Sunday, how many bracelets will she have left over?

(☐ + ☐) − (☐ + ☐) =

⟨Ans.⟩ _____

2 Answer each word problem. Write the question as an expression first, and then calculate. — 10 points per question

(1) To find the area of a square room, Gordon must square the length of one side. The length of one side of room A is $1\frac{1}{4}$ yards. The length of one side of room B is 6 yards. What is the area of both rooms together?

$\left(\square\right)^2 + \square^2 =$

⟨Ans.⟩ _____ yd²

(2) To find the area of a rectangular room, Gordon must multiply the length by the width. The length of room A is 2 yards and the width is $\frac{1}{2}$ yard. Room B is a square, and the length of one side is 4 yards. Room C is the same size as room B. What is the area of all the rooms together?

$\left(\square \times \square\right) + \square^2 + \square^2 =$

⟨Ans.⟩ _____ yd²

3 Answer each word problem. Write the question as an expression first, and then calculate. *15 points per question*

(1) Allison has 4 bags of sugar. Each bag holds $1\frac{5}{8}$ cups. If she combines all of the sugar together in a bowl, and then takes out $1\frac{3}{4}$ cups, how many cups will be in the bowl?

⟨Ans.⟩ _____

(2) Paul has 5 containers of glass beads. Each container holds $2\frac{1}{4}$ cups. He combines all of the beads together in a bowl and then divides the beads evenly into 4 containers. How many cups of beads is in each container?

⟨Ans.⟩ _____

4 Answer each word problem. Write the question as an expression first, and then calculate. *15 points per question*

(1) Jean-Paul bought 2 crates of apples. Each crate weighed $3\frac{5}{6}$ kilograms. He put $1\frac{1}{2}$ kilograms aside for eating and used the rest to bake pies for the bake sale. How many kilograms of apples did he use for the pies?

⟨Ans.⟩ _____

(2) Yesterday, Jan read $\frac{1}{6}$ of his book in the morning and $\frac{1}{4}$ of it in the evening. If he does this again today, how much of his book will he have read?

⟨Ans.⟩ _____

You figured it out!

37 Order of Operations

1 Calculate. Write the intermediate steps. 5 points per question

(1) $3+[4\times(4-1)]\div 2$

$=3+[\square\times\square]\div 2$

$=3+\square\div 2=3+\square=$

(2) $[(2+2^2)\div 3]+4$

$=$

(3) $[8^2\div(2+2)]\div 4$

$=$

(4) $6+24\div(4+2^2)$

$=$

(5) $[27\div(2+1)^2]+4^0$

$=$

(6) $[10\div(8-3)]\times 3^2$

$=$

(7) $[90\div(8-5)^2]-2^2$

$=$

(8) $[42\div(3+3)]-8^2\div 16+2$

$=$

(9) $[96\div(4^2-4)]+(54-3^2)$

$=$

(10) $[(5+1)^2\div 4]-2+45\div 3^2$

$=$

Always calculate from inside to outside and left to right. Perform multiplication and division before addition and subtraction.

2 Calculate. Write the intermediate steps.

5 points per question

(1) $4^2 + [8 \times (5-3)]$

=

(2) $[1 + (2^2 - 1)] - 3$

=

(3) $[(8 \div 2)^2 - 8] \div 2$

=

(4) $60 \div 12 + (8^2 - 5^2)$

=

(5) $8 - [24 \div (4 + 4^2 \div 2)]$

=

(6) $[10 \div (3+2)] \times (8-5)^2$

=

(7) $[15 \div (13-8)]^3 \div 9 + 2$

=

(8) $[(5-2)^2 - 45 \div 3^2] + 1$

=

(9) $45 \div 3^2 \times [(7-5) \times 2]^2$

=

(10) $42 \div 7 - [(6+2)^2 \div 16]$

=

You did it in the correct order!

38 Order of Operations

1 Calculate. Write the intermediate steps.   6 points per question

(1) $\left(\dfrac{3}{4}\right)^2 + (7 \times 5 - 3)$

$= \left(\dfrac{\square}{\square} \times \dfrac{\square}{\square}\right) + (\square - 3) = \dfrac{\square}{\square} + \square =$

(2) $3 \div \left(\dfrac{2}{5} + 2^3\right) + 4$

$=$

(3) $\left(\dfrac{2}{5} + \dfrac{2}{5}\right)^2 + 2^5 \div 8$

$=$

(4) $6 \times \left(1\dfrac{1}{2} - \dfrac{2}{3}\right) + 3^2$

$=$

(5) $\left(\dfrac{1}{2}\right)^2 \times 20 + 1\dfrac{1}{5} \times 5^2$

$=$

(6) $\left(\dfrac{1}{2} \times 1\dfrac{1}{5}\right) \times (80 \div 2^2)$

$=$

(7) $\left(\dfrac{1}{5} + \dfrac{3}{4} - \dfrac{3}{10}\right) \times 2^2$

$=$

(8) $\left(\dfrac{1}{4} - \dfrac{1}{6}\right) \times (5^2 - 1)$

$=$

(9) $\left(\dfrac{3}{16} \times 8 + \dfrac{1}{2}\right) \div 24$

$=$

(10) $\left(\dfrac{1}{4} + \dfrac{7}{8}\right)^2 + 5 \div 2 + 2^2$

$=$

76 © Kumon Publishing Co., Ltd.

2 Calculate. Write the intermediate steps.

5 points per question

(1) $\dfrac{3}{4^2}+[7\times(5-3)]=\dfrac{3}{\Box\times\Box}+[7\times2]$

$=$

(2) $5\div\left[\left(\dfrac{2}{5}\right)^2\div\dfrac{4}{15}\right]\div\dfrac{1}{4}$

$=$

(3) $\left[(3\times2)^2\times\left(1\dfrac{2}{3}-\dfrac{1}{2}\right)\right]+3^2$

$=$

(4) $\left[\left(1\dfrac{1}{2}\right)^3\times4^2\right]\div3^2$

$=$

(5) $\left[\left(1\dfrac{2}{5}\right)^2-\dfrac{9}{25}\right]\times5^2\times\dfrac{1}{2^2}$

$=$

(6) $\left[\left(\dfrac{3}{4}-\dfrac{1}{6}\right)^2\div\dfrac{7}{8}\right]+4^2$

$=$

(7) $\left(2\dfrac{1}{2}\right)^2\times\left(2+1\dfrac{3}{5}\right)$

$=$

(8) $\left(7\dfrac{7}{10}-2\dfrac{1}{5}+4\dfrac{3}{4}\right)\div\dfrac{1}{2^2}$

$=$

Keep up the good work!

39 Order of Operations

1 Calculate. Write the intermediate steps. *8 points per question*

(1) $\left(1\dfrac{1}{2}\right)^3 \div \dfrac{3}{4} + 5.5$

=

(2) $\left(3\dfrac{4}{5} - 2.8 \times \dfrac{4}{7}\right) + 0.4$

=

(3) $\left(\dfrac{2}{9}\right)^2 \times \left(1.7 - 1\dfrac{1}{4}\right)$

=

(4) $7.6 \div \left(2\dfrac{1}{5} - \dfrac{14}{15}\right) + 2^3$

=

(5) $\left(\dfrac{2}{3}\right)^2 \times \left(2\dfrac{7}{8} + 1\dfrac{2}{5}\right) \div 0.3$

=

Convert decimals to fractions in order to calculate.

2 Calculate. Write the intermediate steps.

10 points per question

(1) $1\frac{5}{9} \times \left[\left(\frac{19}{20} - 0.65\right)^2 \div \frac{3}{20}\right]$

=

(2) $\left[3 \times \left(1\frac{1}{3} - \frac{1}{4}\right) \div 1\frac{1}{12}\right]^3$

=

(3) $\left[(3.75 \div 5)^2 + 3\frac{3}{8}\right] - 2.25$

=

(4) $\left[\left(3\frac{3}{4} \div 3\right) \times 0.8\right]^2 + 3\frac{1}{8}$

=

(5) $\left[\left(2\frac{3}{10} + 1\frac{3}{5}\right) \div 0.6 + 6\right] \div 5$

=

(6) $4\frac{3}{8} \times \frac{3}{5} \div \left[\left(\frac{5}{8} - 0.375 + 5\right) \div 3^2\right]$

=

This is hard, but you're doing great!

Order of Operations

1 Calculate. Write the intermediate steps.   8 points per question

(1) $2\dfrac{2}{9} \div \left[\left(\dfrac{17}{20} - 0.55\right)^2 \div 0.54\right]$

$=$

(2) $(0.4)^2 \times \left[\left(\dfrac{1}{2}\right)^2 \times 2^3 \times 3 \div 4\right]^2$

$=$

(3) $\left(2\dfrac{1}{2}\right)^2 \times \left[\left(\dfrac{5}{6}\right)^2 \div 15\right] \div \left(\dfrac{5}{12}\right)^2$

$=$

(4) $\left[1\dfrac{3}{5} + 5^3 \div \left(2\dfrac{1}{2}\right)^2\right] \div 2\dfrac{2}{5}$

$=$

(5) $\left[\left(3\dfrac{3}{4} \div 3\right)^2 \times 0.8\right]^2 - \left[1\dfrac{1}{8} - \left(\dfrac{3}{4}\right)^2\right]$

$=$

2 Calculate. Write the intermediate steps.

10 points per question

(1) $\left[2\times\left(1\frac{1}{3}-0.25\right)\div 1\frac{1}{12}\right]^2$

=

(2) $\left[\left(3\frac{3}{4}\div 5\right)^2+3.375\right]-2\frac{5}{8}$

=

(3) $\left(2\frac{1}{2}\right)^2\times\left[\left(\frac{5}{6}\right)^2\times 1\frac{1}{15}\right]\div\left(1\frac{2}{3}\right)^2$

=

(4) $\left[2\frac{4}{5}-2\frac{2}{9}\times\left(\frac{1}{2}-0.35\right)^2\right]\div 5\frac{1}{2}$

=

(5) $\left[\left(2.3+1\frac{3}{5}\right)\div\frac{3}{5}-1^2\right]\div 5\frac{1}{2}$

=

(6) $(6^2-5^2+2)\div\left(3+\frac{1}{2^2}\right)$

=

Bravo!

Order of Operations 41

1 Calculate. Write the intermediate steps.   8 points per question

(1) $\left[(3.75 \div 5)^2 + 4\dfrac{3}{8}\right] - 0.625$

=

(2) $\left[3 \times \left(2\dfrac{1}{4} - 1.25\right) \div 1\dfrac{1}{4}\right]^2$

=

(3) $3\dfrac{2}{3} \div \left[2.7 - 3\dfrac{1}{8} \times \left(\dfrac{3}{4} - 0.35\right)^2\right]$

=

(4) $(3^3 - 2 \times 7) \div \left[3 + \left(\dfrac{1}{2}\right)^2\right]$

=

(5) $3^2 \times \left(4\dfrac{1}{3} - 3.25\right) \div 1\dfrac{1}{12}$

=

2 Calculate. Write the intermediate steps.   10 points per question

(1) $(5^2 - 12) \div \left[2^2 - 1 + \left(\dfrac{1}{2}\right)^2\right]$

=

(4) $\dfrac{1}{3} \div \left[\left(\dfrac{3}{10}\right)^2 \div 0.54\right]$

=

(2) $\dfrac{2}{3} \times \left[\left(0.65 - \dfrac{7}{20}\right)^2 \div 0.66\right]$

=

(5) $[6^2 - (4^2 - 3)] \div \left(2 + 2\dfrac{3}{5}\right)$

=

(3) $4\dfrac{1}{2} \times [(2.25 + 3) \div 3^2]$

=

(6) $\dfrac{3}{4^2} + (5^2 - 12) \div [3 + (0.5)^2]$

=

You've mastered this!

42 Review

1 Reduce each pair of fractions and compare.

3 points per question

(1) $\dfrac{7}{70} = \dfrac{\ }{\ }$, $\dfrac{9}{30} = \dfrac{\ }{\ }$

$\dfrac{\ }{\square} \dfrac{\ }{\ }$

(2) $\dfrac{15}{27} = \dfrac{\ }{\ }$, $\dfrac{48}{54} = \dfrac{\ }{\ }$

$\dfrac{\ }{\square} \dfrac{\ }{\ }$

(3) $\dfrac{3}{18} = \dfrac{\ }{\ }$, $\dfrac{25}{30} = \dfrac{\ }{\ }$

$\dfrac{\ }{\square} \dfrac{\ }{\ }$

(4) $\dfrac{15}{27} = \dfrac{\ }{\ }$, $\dfrac{14}{63} = \dfrac{\ }{\ }$

$\dfrac{\ }{\square} \dfrac{\ }{\ }$

2 Find the LCM.

2 points per question

(1) (3, 6) → ☐

(2) (8, 12) → ☐

(3) (9, 15) → ☐

(4) (2, 7) → ☐

3 Add.

5 points per question

(1) $\dfrac{1}{2} + \dfrac{3}{5} =$

(2) $\dfrac{1}{2} + \dfrac{3}{5} + \dfrac{1}{6} =$

(3) $1\dfrac{1}{2} + 3\dfrac{3}{4} + \dfrac{1}{8} =$

(4) $1\dfrac{4}{5} + 3\dfrac{3}{8} + 4\dfrac{1}{4} =$

4 Subtract.

5 points per question

(1) $\dfrac{7}{12} - \dfrac{1}{3} =$

(2) $\dfrac{2}{3} - \dfrac{1}{4} =$

(3) $4\dfrac{8}{13} - 2\dfrac{1}{2} =$

(4) $3\dfrac{1}{4} - 1\dfrac{3}{5} =$

5 Calculate.

5 points per question

(1) $\dfrac{7}{12} - \dfrac{1}{4} + \dfrac{1}{3} =$

(2) $\dfrac{11}{12} + 9\dfrac{1}{6} - \dfrac{7}{18} =$

6 Multiply.

5 points per question

(1) $\dfrac{7}{8} \times \dfrac{3}{4} =$

(2) $\dfrac{10}{11} \times \dfrac{22}{25} =$

(3) $5\dfrac{5}{6} \times 2\dfrac{2}{5} =$

(4) $12 \times 1\dfrac{1}{8} \times 1\dfrac{2}{3} =$

7 Divide.

5 points per question

(1) $\dfrac{3}{8} \div \dfrac{1}{4} =$

(2) $2\dfrac{1}{3} \div 1\dfrac{5}{9} =$

You're almost at the finish line!

43 Review

Date / /   Name

Level ★★   Score /100

1 Rewrite each decimal as a fraction or a mixed number. *4 points per question*

(1) $0.18 =$

(2) $0.125 =$

(3) $8.75 =$

(4) $10.55 =$

2 Rewrite each fraction or mixed number as a decimal. *4 points per question*

(1) $\dfrac{4}{5} =$

(2) $\dfrac{3}{50} =$

(3) $1\dfrac{2}{5} =$

(4) $3\dfrac{7}{8} =$

3 Rewrite each decimal as a fraction and a percent. *3 points per question*

(1) $0.35 = \underline{\quad\quad} =$

(2) $0.4805 = \underline{\quad\quad} =$

4 Rewrite each percent as a decimal and a fraction. *3 points per question*

(1) $7\% = \underline{\quad\quad} = \underline{\quad\quad}$

(2) $167.03\% = \underline{\quad\quad} = \underline{\quad\quad}$

5 Rewrite each fraction as a decimal and a percent. *3 points per question*

(1) $\dfrac{2}{5} = \underline{\quad\quad} =$

(2) $2\dfrac{3}{4} = \underline{\quad\quad} =$

86 © Kumon Publishing Co., Ltd.

6 Calculate.

(1) $2.75 - \dfrac{2}{3} =$

(2) $2\dfrac{9}{10} - 2.3 + 1\dfrac{13}{20} =$

7 Calculate.

(1) $\dfrac{5}{8} \div \dfrac{8}{9} \times 0.8 =$

(2) $1.1 \div 1\dfrac{13}{15} \times 2\dfrac{2}{3} =$

8 Calculate.

(1) $5^3 =$

(2) $\left(2\dfrac{1}{2}\right)^2 =$

9 Calculate.

(1) $2^4 \times \dfrac{1}{4^2} =$

(2) $\left(1\dfrac{1}{4}\right)^2 \div 2\dfrac{1}{2} =$

10 Calculate. Write the intermediate steps.

(1) $\left[\left(1\dfrac{2}{3} + 1.75\right) + 3\right] - \dfrac{1}{2^2} =$

(2) $\dfrac{1}{3} \div \left[\left(\dfrac{19}{20} - 0.65\right)^2 \div 0.54\right] =$

Congratulations on completing *Pre-Algebra Workbook 1!*

Answer Key — Grades 6-8 Pre-Algebra Workbook 1

1 Fraction Review — pp 2, 3

①
(1) $1\frac{1}{4}$ (11) 1
(2) $1\frac{2}{5}$ (12) $1\frac{6}{7}$
(3) 1 (13) 2
(4) $2\frac{1}{3}$ (14) 4
(5) $1\frac{3}{4}$ (15) $2\frac{3}{4}$
(6) 2 (16) $4\frac{1}{3}$
(7) $2\frac{1}{2}$ (17) $2\frac{1}{7}$
(8) $2\frac{1}{4}$ (18) 3
(9) $3\frac{1}{3}$ (19) $1\frac{8}{9}$
(10) $1\frac{4}{11}$ (20) $2\frac{4}{7}$

②
(1) $\frac{4}{4}$ (5) $\frac{9}{3}$
(2) $\frac{7}{7}$ (6) $\frac{12}{4}$
(3) $\frac{10}{5}$ (7) $\frac{9}{9}$
(4) $\frac{14}{7}$ (8) $\frac{16}{8}$

③
(1) $\frac{3}{2}$ (7) $\frac{14}{3}$
(2) $\frac{9}{5}$ (8) $\frac{20}{13}$
(3) $\frac{14}{5}$ (9) $\frac{38}{11}$
(4) $\frac{17}{6}$ (10) $\frac{17}{8}$
(5) $\frac{11}{7}$ (11) $\frac{15}{11}$
(6) $\frac{7}{3}$ (12) $\frac{23}{4}$

2 Reduction Review — pp 4, 5

①
(1) $\frac{1}{2}$ (4) $\frac{7}{10}$
(2) $\frac{1}{3}$ (5) $\frac{7}{10}$
(3) $\frac{4}{5}$

②
(1) $\frac{1}{3}$ (4) $\frac{4}{7}$
(2) $\frac{6}{7}$ (5) $\frac{10}{11}$
(3) $\frac{3}{5}$

③
(1) $\frac{1}{2}$ (5) $\frac{5}{6}$
(2) $\frac{3}{4}$ (6) $\frac{1}{3}$
(3) $\frac{5}{7}$ (7) $\frac{5}{11}$
(4) $\frac{5}{7}$ (8) $\frac{1}{4}$

④
(1) $\frac{3}{5}$ (8) $\frac{7}{15}$
(2) $\frac{5}{6}$ (9) $\frac{1}{3}$
(3) $\frac{1}{7}$ (10) $\frac{1}{3}$
(4) $\frac{1}{2}$ (11) $\frac{2}{5}$
(5) $\frac{1}{3}$ (12) $\frac{3}{8}$
(6) $\frac{1}{2}$
(7) $\frac{3}{7}$

3 Greatest Common Factor — pp 6, 7

①
(1) 8
(2) 5
(3) 4
(4) 6
(5) 12
(6) 6

②
(1) 4
(2) 12

③
(1) 6 (3) 14
(2) 5 (4) 9

④
(1) $12, \frac{1}{2}$ (11) $12, \frac{3}{4}$
(2) $4, \frac{4}{5}$ (12) $10, \frac{2}{7}$
(3) $4, \frac{4}{7}$ (13) $11, \frac{2}{5}$
(4) $7, \frac{2}{5}$ (14) $5, \frac{7}{12}$
(5) $15, \frac{1}{2}$ (15) $23, \frac{1}{2}$
(6) $10, \frac{1}{4}$ (16) $5, \frac{5}{13}$
(7) $18, \frac{1}{2}$ (17) $7, \frac{2}{3}$
(8) $3, \frac{3}{11}$ (18) $9, \frac{2}{5}$
(9) $8, \frac{1}{7}$ (19) $10, \frac{2}{9}$
(10) $9, \frac{1}{6}$ (20) $29, \frac{1}{3}$

4 Comparing Fractions — pp 8, 9

①
(1) $\frac{4}{5}, \frac{3}{5}$ (6) $\frac{2}{13}, \frac{8}{13}$
$\frac{4}{5} > \frac{3}{5}$ $\frac{2}{13} < \frac{8}{13}$
(2) $\frac{1}{10}, \frac{3}{10}$ (7) $\frac{1}{6}, \frac{5}{6}$
$\frac{1}{10} < \frac{3}{10}$ $\frac{1}{6} < \frac{5}{6}$
(3) $\frac{11}{15}, \frac{7}{15}$ (8) $\frac{4}{7}, \frac{4}{7}$
$\frac{11}{15} > \frac{7}{15}$ $\frac{4}{7} = \frac{4}{7}$
(4) $\frac{5}{9}, \frac{8}{9}$ (9) $\frac{5}{9}, \frac{2}{9}$
$\frac{5}{9} < \frac{8}{9}$ $\frac{5}{9} > \frac{2}{9}$
(5) $\frac{3}{7}, \frac{3}{7}$ (10) $\frac{7}{12}, \frac{11}{12}$
$\frac{3}{7} = \frac{3}{7}$ $\frac{7}{12} < \frac{11}{12}$

②
(1) $\frac{2}{3} > \frac{1}{3}$ (4) $\frac{6}{13} > \frac{2}{13}$
(2) $\frac{2}{5} = \frac{2}{5}$ (5) $\frac{5}{8} > \frac{3}{8}$
(3) $\frac{1}{4} < \frac{3}{4}$ (6) $\frac{4}{7} = \frac{4}{7}$

③
(1) $\frac{15}{16} > \frac{12}{16}$
Ans. Amanda
(2) $\frac{12}{36}, \frac{18}{27} \rightarrow \frac{1}{3} < \frac{2}{3}$
Ans. Joey

5 Least Common Multiple — pp 10, 11

① $16, 20, 24, 28, 32, 36$
② $24, 30, 36, 42, 48, 54$
③ $21, 28, 35, 42, 49, 56, 63$

(4) 18, 27, 36, 45, 54, 63, 72, 81

(5) 12, 24, 36

(6) 18, 36, 54

(7) 28

(8) (1) 12
(2) 18
(3) 28
(4) 36

(9) (1) 24 (9) 36
(2) 20 (10) 30
(3) 18 (11) 56
(4) 12 (12) 45
(5) 24 (13) 33
(6) 12 (14) 14
(7) 24 (15) 63
(8) 35 (16) 60

6 Comparing Fractions — pp 12, 13

(1) (1) 12 (5) 12
$\frac{4}{12} < \frac{6}{12}$ $\frac{2}{12} < \frac{5}{12}$

(2) 20 (6) 33
$\frac{15}{20} > \frac{14}{20}$ $\frac{22}{33} < \frac{24}{33}$

(3) 24 (7) 60
$\frac{9}{24} < \frac{10}{24}$ $\frac{48}{60} > \frac{35}{60}$

(4) 35 (8) 10
$\frac{14}{35} < \frac{30}{35}$ $\frac{8}{10} < \frac{9}{10}$

(2) (1) $\frac{3}{12} < \frac{10}{12}$ (4) $\frac{15}{18} > \frac{14}{18}$

(2) $\frac{27}{45} < \frac{35}{45}$ (5) $\frac{21}{28} > \frac{12}{28}$

(3) $\frac{40}{45} > \frac{36}{45}$ (6) $\frac{13}{26} > \frac{6}{26}$

(3) (1) $\frac{5}{7}, \frac{10}{11}$ $\frac{55}{77} < \frac{70}{77}$
Ans. Leah

(2) $\frac{3}{4}, \frac{8}{9}$ $\frac{27}{36} < \frac{32}{36}$
Ans. Mrs. Castamore's dance class

7 Addition of Fractions — pp 14, 15

(1) (1) $\frac{4}{5}$ (7) $\frac{8}{9}$
(2) 1 (8) $1\frac{2}{11}$
(3) $1\frac{2}{7}$ (9) 1
(4) $1\frac{4}{9}$ (10) $1\frac{1}{3}$
(5) $1\frac{2}{3}$ (11) $1\frac{4}{5}$
(6) $1\frac{1}{2}$ (12) $1\frac{1}{2}$

(2) (1) 18 (6) 30
(2) 15 (7) 40
(3) 36 (8) 42
(4) 30 (9) 30
(5) 16 (10) 36

(3) (1) 12, $\frac{7}{12}$ (4) 36, $\frac{29}{36}$
(2) 24, $\frac{19}{24}$ (5) 24, $\frac{23}{24}$
(3) 56, $\frac{45}{56}$ (6) 45, $\frac{41}{45}$

8 Addition of Fractions — pp 16, 17

(1) (1) $\frac{17}{21}$ (7) $\frac{11}{18}$
(2) $\frac{23}{30}$ (8) $1\frac{7}{40}$
(3) $1\frac{3}{56}$ (9) $\frac{7}{12}$
(4) $1\frac{23}{42}$ (10) $1\frac{13}{24}$
(5) $1\frac{18}{35}$ (11) $1\frac{1}{28}$
(6) $\frac{11}{12}$ (12) $1\frac{3}{10}$

(2) (1) $1\frac{2}{15}$ (8) $\frac{9}{20}$
(2) $\frac{5}{6}$ (9) $1\frac{1}{2}$
(3) $1\frac{11}{21}$ (10) $\frac{29}{56}$
(4) $1\frac{1}{8}$ (11) $\frac{31}{42}$
(5) $1\frac{1}{24}$ (12) $\frac{13}{15}$
(6) $\frac{19}{24}$ (13) $\frac{7}{8}$
(7) $1\frac{5}{12}$

9 Addition of Fractions — pp 18, 19

(1) (1) $\frac{2}{12} + \frac{4}{12} + \frac{6}{12} = \frac{12}{12} = 1$ (6) $1\frac{7}{60}$
(2) $1\frac{13}{30}$ (7) $1\frac{1}{36}$
(3) $1\frac{11}{18}$ (8) $1\frac{17}{40}$
(4) $2\frac{1}{5}$ (9) $1\frac{23}{44}$
(5) $1\frac{17}{18}$ (10) $1\frac{1}{5}$

(2) (1) $1\frac{14}{15}$ (6) $4\frac{11}{24}$
(2) $1\frac{4}{8} + 3\frac{6}{8} + 1\frac{1}{8} = 5\frac{3}{8}$ (7) $5\frac{1}{12}$
(3) $3\frac{2}{3}$ (8) $4\frac{1}{12}$
(4) $3\frac{59}{70}$ (9) $4\frac{5}{36}$
(5) $9\frac{17}{40}$ (10) $3\frac{5}{8}$

10 Subtraction of Fractions — pp 20, 21

(1) (1) $\frac{2}{7}$ (6) $\frac{1}{5}$
(2) $\frac{1}{2}$ (7) $\frac{1}{6}$
(3) $\frac{2}{3}$ (8) $\frac{1}{3}$
(4) $\frac{5}{13}$ (9) $\frac{3}{10}$
(5) $\frac{5}{11}$ (10) $\frac{5}{12}$

(2) (1) $\frac{5}{12}$ (6) $2\frac{1}{12}$
(2) $\frac{1}{4}$ (7) $1\frac{3}{10}$
(3) $\frac{3}{22}$ (8) $2\frac{1}{3}$
(4) $2\frac{14}{22} - 1\frac{11}{22} = 1\frac{3}{22}$ (9) $2\frac{5}{18}$
(5) $2\frac{8}{21}$ (10) $1\frac{8}{15}$

11 Subtraction of Fractions
pp 22, 23

1
(1) $3\frac{\boxed{5}}{20} - 1\frac{\boxed{12}}{20} = 2\frac{\boxed{25}}{20} - 1\frac{\boxed{12}}{20} = 1\frac{13}{20}$
(2) $2\frac{19}{21}$
(3) $3\frac{11}{14}$
(4) $2\frac{7}{10}$
(5) $2\frac{13}{22}$
(6) $1\frac{23}{26}$
(7) $4\frac{13}{16}$
(8) $\frac{27}{44}$
(9) $1\frac{5}{14}$
(10) $\frac{7}{20}$

2
(1) $\frac{\boxed{11}}{12} - \frac{\boxed{3}}{12} - \frac{\boxed{4}}{12} = \frac{4}{12} = \frac{1}{3}$
(2) $\frac{1}{7}$
(3) $2\frac{7}{24}$
(4) $3\frac{7}{24}$
(5) $5\frac{3}{4}$
(6) $2\frac{7}{18}$
(7) $2\frac{1}{24}$
(8) $3\frac{5}{24}$
(9) $2\frac{5}{36}$
(10) $\frac{7}{8}$

12 Addition & Subtraction of Fractions
pp 24, 25

1
(1) $\frac{\boxed{8}}{18} + \frac{\boxed{9}}{18} - \frac{\boxed{12}}{18} = \frac{5}{18}$
(2) $\frac{2}{3}$
(3) $4\frac{1}{18}$
(4) $2\frac{1}{2}$
(5) $9\frac{8}{45}$
(6) $5\frac{3}{5}$
(7) $7\frac{1}{3}$
(8) $1\frac{2}{3}$
(9) $11\frac{5}{18}$
(10) $10\frac{13}{21}$

2
(1) $\frac{7}{8}$
(2) $2\frac{7}{12}$
(3) $7\frac{1}{3}$
(4) $3\frac{17}{18}$
(5) $8\frac{31}{36}$
(6) $7\frac{3}{28}$
(7) $1\frac{7}{12}$
(8) $1\frac{9}{10}$
(9) $1\frac{5}{24}$
(10) $2\frac{19}{72}$

13 Word Problems with Fractions
pp 26, 27

1
(1) $\frac{4}{10} + \frac{1}{10} = \frac{5}{10} = \frac{1}{2}$　　Ans. $\frac{1}{2}$ liter
(2) $\frac{1}{9} + \frac{1}{3} = \frac{1}{9} + \frac{3}{9} = \frac{4}{9}$　　Ans. $\frac{4}{9}$ meter
(3) $\frac{3}{6} + \frac{4}{6} + \frac{1}{6} = \frac{8}{6} = 1\frac{2}{6} = 1\frac{1}{3}$　　Ans. $1\frac{1}{3}$ kilometers
(4) $1\frac{1}{3} + \frac{1}{2} + 2\frac{5}{6} = 1\frac{2}{6} + \frac{3}{6} + 2\frac{5}{6} = 3\frac{10}{6} = 4\frac{4}{6} = 4\frac{2}{3}$

Ans. $4\frac{2}{3}$ cups

2
(1) $3\frac{3}{4} - 1\frac{2}{5} = 3\frac{\boxed{15}}{20} - 1\frac{\boxed{8}}{20} = 2\frac{7}{20}$　　Ans. $2\frac{7}{20}$ pounds
(2) $2\frac{8}{9} - 1\frac{1}{3} = 2\frac{8}{9} - 1\frac{3}{9} = 1\frac{5}{9}$　　Ans. $1\frac{5}{9}$ cups
(3) $8\frac{4}{15} - 5\frac{7}{10} - 1\frac{1}{5} = 1\frac{11}{30}$　　Ans. $1\frac{11}{30}$ ounces
(4) $15\frac{3}{4} - 8\frac{7}{12} - 2\frac{1}{3} = 4\frac{5}{6}$　　Ans. $4\frac{5}{6}$ gallons

3
(1) $1\frac{7}{15} - \frac{4}{5} + \frac{1}{3} = 1$　　Ans. 1 pound
(2) $4\frac{1}{6} - \frac{5}{12} + \frac{1}{2} = 4\frac{1}{4}$　　Ans. $4\frac{1}{4}$ pages

14 Multiplication of Fractions
pp 28, 29

1
(1) $\frac{\boxed{1}}{12}$
(2) $\frac{18}{35}$
(3) $\frac{16}{63}$
(4) $\frac{8}{25}$
(5) $\frac{21}{32}$
(6) $\frac{20}{63}$
(7) $\frac{14}{27}$
(8) $\frac{11}{26}$
(9) $\frac{11}{48}$
(10) $\frac{25}{84}$

2
(1) $\frac{2}{5}$
(2) $\frac{\boxed{2}}{\underset{\boxed{1}}{\boxed{10}}{11}} \times \frac{\boxed{22}}{\underset{\boxed{5}}{15}} = \frac{\boxed{4}}{5}$
(3) $\frac{4}{27}$
(4) $\frac{5}{44}$
(5) $\frac{9}{50}$
(6) $\frac{5}{6}$
(7) $\frac{2}{3}$
(8) $\frac{21}{23}$
(9) $\frac{3}{44}$
(10) $\frac{5}{8}$

15 Multiplication of Fractions
pp 30, 31

1
(1) $\frac{5}{\underset{\boxed{1}}{3}} \times \frac{\boxed{3}}{\overset{}{4}} = \frac{15}{4} = 3\frac{3}{4}$
(2) $\frac{9}{4} \times \frac{\overset{7}{28}}{13} = \frac{63}{13} = 4\frac{11}{13}$
(3) 18
(4) $8\frac{6}{7}$
(5) $5\frac{1}{4}$
(6) 24
(7) 14
(8) $10\frac{1}{2}$
(9) 35
(10) 9

2
(1) $\frac{1}{6}$
(2) $\frac{2}{15}$
(3) $\frac{4}{5}$
(4) $19\frac{1}{2}$
(5) $27\frac{1}{2}$
(6) $4\frac{1}{4}$
(7) $13\frac{1}{2}$
(8) $\frac{4}{5}$
(9) $22\frac{1}{2}$
(10) $\frac{13}{30}$

16 Division of Fractions
pp 32, 33

1
(1) $\frac{8}{9} \times \frac{\boxed{2}}{1} = \frac{16}{9} = 1\frac{7}{9}$ (6) $\frac{18}{35}$
(2) $\frac{4}{5} \times \frac{\boxed{7}}{3} = \frac{28}{15} = 1\frac{13}{15}$ (7) $1\frac{5}{16}$
(3) $\frac{9}{20}$ (8) $\frac{27}{35}$
(4) $1\frac{17}{18}$ (9) $3\frac{3}{14}$
(5) $\frac{16}{35}$ (10) $2\frac{10}{13}$

2
(1) $1\frac{1}{7}$ (6) $1\frac{1}{2}$
(2) $\frac{2}{3}$ (7) $1\frac{1}{5}$
(3) $1\frac{1}{9}$ (8) $1\frac{1}{14}$
(4) $\frac{5}{7}$ (9) $1\frac{1}{20}$
(5) $\frac{3}{7}$ (10) $\frac{44}{45}$

17 Division of Fractions
pp 34, 35

1
(1) $\frac{1}{7} \times \frac{1}{\boxed{4}} = \frac{1}{28}$ (3) $\frac{3}{40}$ (5) $4\frac{4}{7}$
(2) $\frac{6}{7} \div \frac{\boxed{7}}{1} = \frac{6}{7} \times \frac{1}{7} = \frac{6}{49}$ (4) $\frac{\boxed{5}}{1} \div \frac{1}{4} = \frac{5}{1} \times \frac{4}{1} = 20$

2
(1) $\frac{5}{6}$ (3) 2 (5) $1\frac{1}{2}$
(2) $\frac{8}{33}$ (4) $1\frac{1}{3}$

3
(1) $\frac{4}{27}$ (4) $\frac{2}{45}$
(2) $\frac{4}{5} \div \frac{\boxed{5}}{3} \div \frac{3}{2} = \frac{4}{5} \times \frac{3}{5} \times \frac{2}{3} = \frac{8}{25}$ (5) $1\frac{2}{7}$
(3) $\frac{1}{8}$ (6) $2\frac{5}{8}$

4
(1) 1
(2) $\frac{1}{3}$
(3) $\frac{8}{15}$
(4) 2

18 Word Problems with Fractions
pp 36, 37

1
(1) $1\frac{1}{4} \times 6 = 7\frac{1}{2}$ Ans. $7\frac{1}{2}$ miles
(2) $2\frac{4}{9} \times 12 = 29\frac{1}{3}$ Ans. $29\frac{1}{3}$ pounds
(3) $4\frac{1}{4} \div \frac{2}{3} \times 6 = 38\frac{1}{4}$ Ans. $38\frac{1}{4}$ feet
(4) $3 \times \frac{1}{2} \times \frac{1}{2} = \frac{3}{4}$ Ans. $\frac{3}{4}$ cup

2
(1) $\frac{5}{7} \times \frac{1}{2} = \frac{5}{14}$ Ans. $\frac{5}{14}$ yard
(2) $\frac{6}{7} \div 3 = \frac{6}{7} \times \frac{1}{3} = \frac{2}{7}$ Ans. $\frac{2}{7}$ pound
(3) $12 \div \frac{3}{5} = 20$ Ans. 20 liters
(4) $1\frac{14}{15} \div 2 = \frac{29}{30}$ Ans. $\frac{29}{30}$ liter

19 Fraction Review
pp 38, 39

1
(1) $1\frac{18}{35}$ (4) $1\frac{1}{7}$
(2) $3\frac{59}{70}$ (5) $4\frac{1}{2}$
(3) $2\frac{19}{21}$ (6) $3\frac{8}{45}$

2
(1) $8\frac{6}{7}$ (4) $\frac{11}{36}$
(2) $12\frac{1}{2}$ (5) $18\frac{2}{3}$
(3) $\frac{18}{23}$ (6) $\frac{5}{32}$

3
(1) $1\frac{3}{4} + 1\frac{1}{3} + 1\frac{1}{6} = 4\frac{1}{4}$ Ans. $4\frac{1}{4}$ pounds
(2) $5\frac{1}{9} + 1\frac{1}{3} - 1\frac{5}{18} = 5\frac{1}{6}$ Ans. $5\frac{1}{6}$ cups

4
(1) $4\frac{1}{4} \div \frac{7}{8} \times 4\frac{1}{2} = 21\frac{6}{7}$ Ans. $21\frac{6}{7}$ miles
(2) $7\frac{1}{2} \div 4\frac{1}{6} \times 8\frac{3}{4} = 15\frac{3}{4}$ Ans. $15\frac{3}{4}$ yards

20 Place Value Review
pp 40, 41

1 (1) 4, 6 (2) 2, 4 (3) 8, 2 (4) 9, 3 (5) 7, 4

2
(1) (From the left) 0.1, 0.4, 0.7
(2) 0.07, 0.25, 0.61, 0.85, 0.99
(3) 0.19, 0.36, 0.56, 1.01

3 (1) 6.7 (2) 8.5 (3) 0.2

4 (1) 8.92 (2) 4.45 (3) 0.11

5 (1) 0.157 (2) 0.112 (3) 23.783

6 (1) 0.015 (3) 0.014
(2) 0.015 (4) 0.016

21 Decimals as Fractions
pp 42, 43

1
(1) $\frac{5}{10} = \frac{\boxed{1}}{\boxed{2}}$ (6) $\frac{18}{100} = \frac{9}{\boxed{50}}$
(2) $\frac{8}{10} = \frac{\boxed{4}}{\boxed{5}}$ (7) $\frac{8}{100} = \frac{\boxed{2}}{25}$
(3) $\frac{\boxed{25}}{\boxed{100}} = \frac{1}{4}$ (8) $\frac{5}{\boxed{1000}} = \frac{1}{\boxed{200}}$
(4) $\frac{35}{\boxed{100}} = \frac{7}{\boxed{20}}$ (9) $\frac{825}{\boxed{1000}} = \frac{33}{\boxed{40}}$
(5) $\frac{5}{\boxed{100}} = \frac{1}{\boxed{20}}$ (10) $\frac{404}{\boxed{1000}} = \frac{101}{\boxed{250}}$

91

2 (1) $3\frac{1}{2}$ (4) $2\frac{17}{25}$
(2) $5\frac{3}{4}$ (5) $10\frac{11}{20}$
(3) $2\frac{3}{5}$ (6) $9\frac{1}{200}$

3 (1) $\frac{5}{2}$ (4) $\frac{52}{25}$
(2) $\frac{17}{5}$ (5) $\frac{13}{8}$
(3) $\frac{28}{25}$ (6) $\frac{251}{125}$

22 Fractions as Decimals   pp 44, 45

1 (1) 0.25 $\begin{array}{r}0.25\\4\overline{)1.0}\\\underline{8}\\20\\\underline{20}\\0\end{array}$ (5) 0.06
(2) 0.75   (6) 0.375
(3) 0.8   (7) 8.25
(4) 1.4   (8) 7.75

2 (1) 2.25   (5) 3.62   (9) 7.875
(2) 7.8   (6) 10.2   (10) 2.625
(3) 5.375 (7) 5.48
(4) 4.12   (8) 2.6

23 Percents   pp 46, 47

1 (1) $\boxed{45}$, 45%   (6) 123, 12.3%
(2) 35, 35%   (7) 971, 97.1%
(3) 40, 40%   (8) 979, 97.9%
(4) 4, 4%   (9) 4805, 48.05%
(5) 4, 0.4%   (10) 3, 0.03%

2 (1) 100%   (6) 100.5%
(2) 145%   (7) 101.2%
(3) 104%   (8) 110.3%
(4) 104.5%   (9) 200%
(5) 1047%   (10) 202%

24 Percents   pp 48, 49

1 (1) $\frac{\boxed{45}}{100}=0.45$ (6) $\frac{\boxed{264}}{1000}=0.264$
(2) $\frac{\boxed{55}}{100}=0.55$ (7) $\frac{\boxed{149}}{1000}=0.149$
(3) $\frac{\boxed{70}}{100}=0.7$ (8) $\frac{\boxed{8}}{1000}=0.008$
(4) $\frac{\boxed{87}}{100}=0.87$ (9) $\frac{\boxed{6702}}{10000}=0.6702$
(5) $\frac{\boxed{6}}{100}=0.06$ (10) $\frac{\boxed{9}}{10000}=0.0009$

2 (1) 1   (6) 10
(2) 1.45   (7) 11
(3) 1.08   (8) 11.1
(4) 1.17   (9) 11.11
(5) 1.1   (10) 10.11

25 Percents   pp 50, 51

1 (1) $0.25=\frac{\boxed{25}}{100}=\frac{\boxed{1}}{4}$ (6) $1.5=\frac{15}{10}=\frac{3}{2}=1\frac{1}{2}$
(2) $0.75=\frac{75}{100}=\frac{3}{4}$ (7) $1.25=\frac{125}{100}=\frac{5}{4}=1\frac{1}{4}$
(3) $0.6=\frac{60}{100}=\frac{3}{5}$ (8) $1.05=\frac{105}{100}=\frac{21}{20}=1\frac{1}{20}$
(4) $0.15=\frac{15}{100}=\frac{3}{20}$ (9) $0.105=\frac{105}{1000}=\frac{21}{200}$
(5) $0.26=\frac{26}{100}=\frac{13}{50}$ (10) $1.005=\frac{1005}{1000}=\frac{201}{200}=1\frac{1}{200}$

2 (1) 0.5 = 50%   (4) 0.35 = 35%
(2) 0.25 = 25%   (5) 1.8 = 180%
(3) 0.4 = 40%   (6) 1.75 = 175%

3 (1) 0.82 = 82%   Ans. 82%
(2) 1.47 = 147%   Ans. 147%

4 (1) 8,250% = 82.5   Ans. 82.5
(2) 27% = 0.27   Ans. 0.27

5 (1) $\frac{5}{8}=0.625=62.5\%$ Ans. 62.5%
(2) $\frac{1}{5}=0.2=20\%$ Ans. 20%

26 Decimals and Fractions — pp 52, 53

1)
(1) $\frac{1}{6}+\frac{1}{2}=\frac{4}{6}=\frac{2}{3}$
(2) $\frac{13}{20}$
(3) $1\frac{9}{20}$
(4) $2\frac{1}{3}$
(5) $1\frac{29}{40}$
(6) $\frac{5}{12}$
(7) $\frac{3}{10}$
(8) $\frac{7}{30}$
(9) $2\frac{1}{12}$
(10) $3\frac{7}{20}$

2)
(1) $\frac{9}{10}$
(2) $1\frac{9}{10}$
(3) $\frac{39}{40}$
(4) $5\frac{3}{20}$
(5) $2\frac{17}{20}$
(6) $1\frac{19}{20}$
(7) $\frac{4}{5}$
(8) $\frac{23}{24}$
(9) $1\frac{19}{24}$
(10) $\frac{13}{36}$

27 Decimals and Fractions — pp 54, 55

1)
(1) $\frac{1}{12}$
(2) $\frac{5}{8}$
(3) $\frac{1}{30}$
(4) $2\frac{2}{5}$
(5) $\frac{1}{15}$
(6) $1\frac{4}{5}$
(7) $\frac{11}{18}$
(8) $1\frac{19}{20}$
(9) $8\frac{1}{3}$
(10) $\frac{3}{10}$

2)
(1) $\frac{1}{2}$
(2) $\frac{9}{16}$
(3) $\frac{2}{3}$
(4) $\frac{20}{21}$
(5) $\frac{5}{8}$
(6) $5\frac{5}{8}$
(7) $2\frac{14}{25}$
(8) $2\frac{33}{50}$
(9) $11\frac{1}{5}$
(10) $\frac{17}{25}$

28 Word Problems with Decimals and Fractions — pp 56, 57

1)
(1) $\frac{9}{10}-0.15+\frac{3}{100}=\frac{39}{50}$ — Ans. $\frac{39}{50}$ liter
(2) $6\frac{9}{10}-2.15+\frac{1}{6}=4\frac{11}{12}$ — Ans. $4\frac{11}{12}$ feet

2)
(1) $1\frac{8}{15}\times 4.5=6\frac{9}{10}$ — Ans. $6\frac{9}{10}$ yards
(2) $2.15\times 3\frac{1}{3}=7\frac{1}{6}$ — Ans. $7\frac{1}{6}$ meters

3)
(1) $3\frac{1}{3}\times 2.5\div\frac{5}{6}=10$ — Ans. 10 pieces
(2) $1.2\times 6.75\div\frac{9}{10}=9$ — Ans. 9 pieces

4)
(1) $0.6\times\frac{1}{9}+0.1=\frac{1}{6}$ — Ans. $\frac{1}{6}$ ton
(2) $1.5\times\frac{9}{10}-0.25=1\frac{1}{10}$ — Ans. $1\frac{1}{10}$ liters

29 Exponents — pp 58, 59

1)
(1) 4
(2) 8
(3) 16
(4) 9
(5) 27
(6) 1
(7) 243
(8) 256
(9) 1
(10) 343

2)
(1) $\frac{1}{4}$
(2) $\frac{1}{8}$
(3) $\frac{1}{16}$
(4) $\frac{1}{16}$
(5) $\frac{3}{125}$
(6) 1

3)
(1) $\frac{3}{4}\times\frac{3}{4}\times\frac{3}{4}=\frac{27}{64}$ — Ans. $\frac{27}{64}$ in³
(2) $\frac{4}{5}\times\frac{4}{5}\times\frac{4}{5}=\frac{64}{125}$ — Ans. $\frac{64}{125}$ ft³

30 Exponents — pp 60, 61

1)
(1) $1\frac{7}{9}$
(2) $2\frac{10}{27}$
(3) $3\frac{3}{8}$
(4) $5\frac{1}{16}$
(5) $6\frac{1}{4}$
(6) $2\frac{7}{9}$
(7) $5\frac{1}{16}$
(8) $4\frac{17}{27}$
(9) 1
(10) $14\frac{1}{16}$

2)
(1) 8
(2) $\frac{3}{8}$
(3) 4
(4) $\frac{5}{8}$
(5) 12
(6) 144

3)
(1) $\frac{3}{4}$
(2) $121\frac{1}{2}$
(3) 2500
(4) 256
(5) 225
(6) $\frac{25}{216}$

31 Order of Operations — pp 62, 63

1)
(1) $7-\boxed{5}=2$
(2) 4
(3) 9
(4) 9
(5) 7
(6) 56
(7) 4
(8) 6
(9) 4
(10) 6

2 (1) $\frac{5}{7} - \frac{\boxed{4}}{7} = \frac{1}{7}$ (6) $2\frac{1}{6}$

(2) $\frac{1}{2} + \left(\frac{\boxed{20}}{4} - \frac{1}{4}\right) = 5\frac{1}{4}$ (7) 14

(3) $\frac{2}{3}$ (8) $\frac{3}{4}$

(4) $\frac{2}{5}$ (9) 3

(5) 15 (10) $5\frac{1}{2}$

32 Order of Operations   pp 64, 65

1 (1) $[4+\boxed{7}] - 9 = \boxed{11} - 9 = 2$

(2) 7

(3) 9

(4) 12

(5) $1\frac{1}{6}$

(6) $[\boxed{3} \div \boxed{1}] + \frac{5}{7} = \boxed{3} + \frac{5}{7} = 3\frac{5}{7}$

(7) 3

(8) $3\frac{27}{28}$

(9) 4

(10) $5\frac{6}{7}$

2 (1) $6 - \left[\left(\frac{1}{4} + \frac{\boxed{3}}{\boxed{4}}\right) - \frac{3}{4}\right] = 5\frac{3}{4}$ (6) 6

(2) $4 - \left[\frac{1}{3} + 1\frac{\boxed{1}}{\boxed{10}}\right] = 2\frac{17}{30}$ (7) 6

(3) $\frac{4}{5}$ (or 0.8) (8) 30

(4) $6\frac{1}{2}$ (or 6.5) (9) 10

(5) $7\frac{2}{5}$ (10) $9\frac{1}{15}$

33 Order of Operations   pp 66, 67

1 (1) $3^2 - (4 + \boxed{5}) = 3^2 - \boxed{9} = \boxed{9} - \boxed{9} = 0$

(2) 32

(3) 19

(4) 2

(5) $[2 + (\boxed{9} - 4)] \times \frac{5}{7} = [2 + \boxed{5}] \times \frac{5}{7} = 5$

(6) $\frac{6}{7}$

(7) $8\frac{3}{16}$

(8) $3\frac{1}{2}$

2 (1) $16\frac{5}{18}$ (6) 6

(2) $11\frac{25}{49}$ (7) $6\frac{11}{20}$

(3) 3 (8) $51\frac{7}{9}$

(4) $\frac{2}{3}$ (9) $5\frac{9}{64}$

(5) $\frac{11}{81}$ (10) 32

34 Order of Operations   pp 68, 69

1 (1) $8\frac{1}{4}$ (5) 10

(2) $14\frac{7}{12}$ (6) $9\frac{3}{5}$

(3) 8 (7) 36

(4) $16\frac{23}{36}$ (8) 8

2 (1) 18 (4) 2

(2) 10 (5) $9\frac{1}{8}$

(3) $13\frac{1}{24}$ (6) 27

35 Order of Operations   pp 70,71

1
(1) $6 - \boxed{4} = 2$
(2) 10
(3) 11
(4) $\frac{2}{3} + \frac{\boxed{2}}{\boxed{3}} = \frac{4}{3} = 1\frac{1}{3}$
(5) $7\frac{3}{4}$
(6) 2
(7) 10
(8) $9\frac{1}{2}$
(9) $2\frac{2}{9}$
(10) $1\frac{1}{6}$

2
(1) $1\frac{1}{2}$
(2) $1\frac{1}{2}$
(3) $1\frac{7}{10}$
(4) $3\frac{1}{3}$
(5) $9\frac{1}{3}$
(6) $\frac{29}{30}$
(7) $\frac{3}{4}$
(8) $2\frac{1}{7}$
(9) 7
(10) $\frac{1}{2}$

36 Word Problems with Order of Operations   pp 72,73

1
(1) $\boxed{15} - (\boxed{16} - \boxed{3}) = 15 - 13 = 2$ **Ans.** 2 cupcakes
(2) $(\boxed{8} + \boxed{8}) - (\boxed{9} + \boxed{5}) = 16 - 14 = 2$ **Ans.** 2 bracelets

2
(1) $\boxed{1\frac{1}{4}}^2 + \boxed{6}^2 = 37\frac{9}{16}$ **Ans.** $37\frac{9}{16}$ yd²
(2) $(\boxed{2} \times \boxed{\frac{1}{2}}) + \boxed{4}^2 + \boxed{4}^2 = 33$ **Ans.** 33 yd²

3
(1) $1\frac{5}{8} \times 4 - 1\frac{3}{4} = 4\frac{3}{4}$ **Ans.** $4\frac{3}{4}$ cups
(2) $2\frac{1}{4} \times 5 \div 4 = 2\frac{13}{16}$ **Ans.** $2\frac{13}{16}$ cups

4
(1) $2 \times 3\frac{5}{6} - 1\frac{1}{2} = 6\frac{1}{6}$ **Ans.** $6\frac{1}{6}$ kilograms
(2) $(\frac{1}{6} + \frac{1}{4}) \times 2 = \frac{5}{6}$ **Ans.** $\frac{5}{6}$ of his book

37 Order of Operations   pp 74,75

1
(1) $3 + [\boxed{4} \times \boxed{3}] \div 2 = 3 + \boxed{12} \div 2 = 3 + \boxed{6} = 9$
(2) 6
(3) 4
(4) 9
(5) 4
(6) 18
(7) 6
(8) 5
(9) 53
(10) 12

2
(1) 32
(2) 1
(3) 4
(4) 44
(5) 6
(6) 18
(7) 5
(8) 5
(9) 80
(10) 2

38 Order of Operations   pp 76,77

1
(1) $(\frac{\boxed{3}}{\boxed{4}} \times \frac{\boxed{3}}{\boxed{4}}) + (\boxed{35} - 3) = \frac{9}{\boxed{16}} + \boxed{32} = 32\frac{9}{16}$
(2) $4\frac{5}{14}$
(3) $4\frac{16}{25}$
(4) 14
(5) 35
(6) 12
(7) $2\frac{3}{5}$
(8) 2
(9) $\frac{1}{12}$
(10) $7\frac{49}{64}$

2
(1) $\frac{3}{\boxed{4} \times \boxed{4}} + [7 \times 2] = 14\frac{3}{16}$
(2) $33\frac{1}{3}$
(3) 51
(4) 6
(5) 10
(6) $16\frac{7}{18}$
(7) $22\frac{1}{2}$
(8) 41

39 Order of Operations   pp 78,79

1
(1) 10
(2) $2\frac{3}{5}$
(3) $\frac{1}{45}$
(4) 14
(5) $6\frac{1}{3}$

2
(1) $\frac{14}{15}$
(2) 27
(3) $1\frac{11}{16}$
(4) $4\frac{1}{8}$
(5) $2\frac{1}{2}$
(6) $4\frac{1}{2}$

40 Order of Operations   pp 80,81

1
(1) $13\frac{1}{3}$
(2) $\frac{9}{25}$
(3) $1\frac{2}{3}$
(4) 9
(5) 1

2
(1) 4
(2) $1\frac{5}{16}$
(3) $1\frac{2}{3}$
(4) $\frac{1}{2}$
(5) 1
(6) 4

41 Order of Operations   pp 82, 83

1 (1) $4\frac{5}{16}$ (4) 4
(2) $5\frac{19}{25}$ (5) 9
(3) $1\frac{2}{3}$

2 (1) 4 (4) 2
(2) $\frac{1}{11}$ (5) 5
(3) $2\frac{5}{8}$ (6) $4\frac{3}{16}$

42 Review   pp 84, 85

1 (1) $\frac{1}{10}, \frac{3}{10}$ (3) $\frac{1}{6}, \frac{5}{6}$
$\frac{1}{10} < \frac{3}{10}$ $\frac{1}{6} < \frac{5}{6}$
(2) $\frac{5}{9}, \frac{8}{9}$ (4) $\frac{5}{9}, \frac{2}{9}$
$\frac{5}{9} < \frac{8}{9}$ $\frac{5}{9} > \frac{2}{9}$

2 (1) 6 (3) 45
(2) 24 (4) 14

3 (1) $1\frac{1}{10}$ (3) $5\frac{3}{8}$
(2) $1\frac{4}{15}$ (4) $9\frac{17}{40}$

4 (1) $\frac{1}{4}$ (3) $2\frac{3}{26}$
(2) $\frac{5}{12}$ (4) $1\frac{13}{20}$

5 (1) $\frac{2}{3}$ (2) $9\frac{25}{36}$

6 (1) $\frac{21}{32}$ (3) 14
(2) $\frac{4}{5}$ (4) $22\frac{1}{2}$

7 (1) $1\frac{1}{2}$ (2) $1\frac{1}{2}$

43 Review   pp 86, 87

1 (1) $\frac{9}{50}$ (3) $8\frac{3}{4}$
(2) $\frac{1}{8}$ (4) $10\frac{11}{20}$

2 (1) 0.8 (3) 1.4
(2) 0.06 (4) 3.875

3 (1) $\frac{35}{100} = 35\%$ (2) $\frac{4805}{10000} = 48.05\%$

4 (1) $0.07 = \frac{7}{100}$ (2) $1.6703 = \frac{16703}{10000}$

5 (1) $0.4 = 40\%$ (2) $2.75 = 275\%$

6 (1) $2\frac{1}{12}$ (2) $2\frac{1}{4}$

7 (1) $\frac{9}{16}$ (2) $1\frac{4}{7}$

8 (1) 125 (2) $6\frac{1}{4}$

9 (1) 1 (2) $\frac{5}{8}$

10 (1) $6\frac{1}{6}$ (2) 2